PENN CENTRAL POWER

by

Robert J. Yanosey

Copyright 1987 by

Morning Sun Books, Inc.

Printed by
Crusader Printing

Published by
MORNING SUN BOOKS, Inc.
11 Sussex Court
Edison, N.J. 08820

First Edition
ISBN # 0-9619058-0-8

Front and Rear Photo Data: All by R. J. Yanosey

Page 1: E7 4244 and GG-1 4883 at South Amboy, N.J. motor pit, August 1978.

Page 4: Southbound E8 drawn NY&LB passenger train South Amboy, May 1976.

Page 6: SD45 6172 leads piggyback traffic west at "MG" Tower, east of Gallitzin, Pa. May 1975.

Page 8: Power displays at Kearny, N.J. (top) May 1976, (bottom) November 1974.

Page 9: SD40 6269 and mate start downhill and westward at "MO" Tower, Cresson, Pa. May, 1975.

Page 10: PRR 1457 F7 at Cresson, Pa. August 1967.

Page 11: NYC 1829 F7 at Weehawken, N.J. March 1968.

Page 12: PC (NH) 5030 FL9 at Brewster, N.Y. September 1974.

Page 13: PC 4345 FP7 at Youngwood, Pa. August 1974.

Page 14: PC SD45 6177 and EL SD45 3664 pull a westbound freight thru the Altoona, Pa. yards and past ex PC 7147 newly painted Conrail in that city's shops.

Page 15: (Top) PC E8's await the evening rush hour at South Amboy, N.J. November 1974. (Bottom) Electric locomotives of Virginian, Pennsylvania, and New Haven Railroads' heritage await the night, and tonnage for the west and south.

Page 241: Selkirk, N.Y. engine terminal in October 1973.

Page 244: PC 6025 leads eastbound TV traffic past "Mifflin" tower in the central Pennsylvania town of the same name. This was in May 1975, just three months after the February activity outlined on pages 246-247.

Page 248: SD40 6277 passes over a sign celebrating America's BiCentennial Year 1976; the year Penn Central disappeared into railroad history. Cresson, Pa. August 1976.

Dedication

This book is dedicated to my Dad, Stephen Yanosey, who as a teenager in the 1920's spent countless hours hanging around the PRR tower in Bradenville, Pa. watching and listening in the days before such interest was organized enough to be published in a book.

Acknowledgements

My sincere appreciation is extended to the many people who contributed their efforts to make this book "happen." Thanks to my friend Paul E. Butterworth, Charlie Horan, John Komanesky, Bill Sprague, Paul Kuehner, Frank Fuccello, John Johnson, Don Walker, George DeLuca, Rick Orlowski, Bonner Smith, Bob McKee, Meredyth Patterson, John Scala, Scott Conderman and Bob Giles who all helped in one way or another with information, photos or sound counsel. And recognition must also be given to Kay and Joe Orlowski for nurturing my interest in PRR & PC year after year.

I especially want to acknowledge Marty Zak, Herb Harwood, Jack Swanberg, Bob Malinoski, and my good friend Bill Brennan who opened their negative collections to me completely and followed up with plenty of intriguing information about their fine shots.

Mark Branibar spent long hours compiling a real, all time roster of Penn Central Power. Previous rosters were based on the 1966 renumbering or were written before all the new power and renumberings had taken place. Your efforts are well appreciated, Mark. Of course, the most special gratitude is reserved for my wonderful wife Michele. It is *only* through her patience and understanding that I can undertake such a project as this one.

Thank you, all of you.

Table of Contents

Penn Central's Brief History

Once I built a railroad, made it run — Made it race against time.
Once I built a railroad, Now it's done — Brother, can you spare a dime?

—"Brother, Can You Spare A Dime?" words by
E.Y. Harburg © 1932 Warner Bros. (Renewed)

At the stroke of midnight February 1, 1968, the history of railroading in the United States began its greatest change since the steam engine relinquished its reign to the diesel some 15 years earlier. At that moment in time, the two historically greatest railroads in this land consumated a marriage which was supposed to produce a company equal to the challenges of the 1970's, and even the 21st century. The Pennsylvania and New York Central Railroads had prospered for over 100 years, paying dividends and earning a fixed place in the proverbial "widow's portfolio." Tragically, the product of their spawning, the Penn Central* Railroad, was to retain its "solvency" only a little more than two years before crashing in a bankruptcy that would change the face of American railroading forever more.

The Pennsylvania Railroad, created in 1846, had flourished during the first century of its existence. Its conservative presidents reinvested the profits of their company's toils and built the oft referred to, "Standard Railroad of the World." More flamboyant, perhaps because of its Vanderbilt heritage, the New York Central also enjoyed fiscal health during this period and came to enjoy the operating efficiencies inherent in a well tracked "Water Level Route." Both roads were essentially east - west trunk lines with numerous branch lines and deeply ensconced in the passenger business of the heavily populated eastern states. While other firms failed during the Great Depression of the thirties, the two companies pressed on and performed yeoman duties during the Second World War. With Peace, the two giants began to stagger for the first time. The PRR was embarrassed in its 1946 Centennial Anniversary by having to report an annual loss for the first time in its history. NYC, more geared to large scale passenger operations and general merchandise traffic, became mired in a sea of red ink during this period and was only able to stop the hemorrhaging after a nasty battle for control of the line brought in new management. Both roads limped into the 1960's with too much capacity, debt, passenger service, and marginal profits. The future appeared bleak when the freight traffic trend worsened as the trucking industry became invigorated by the newly completed interstate highway system. Passenger service, already in a long downward spiral was delivered the coup de grace by the Eisenhower highway program and an airline system that started to come into its own with new jets and modern airports. Losses in commuter service continued to rise as inflation, ever higher labor costs, and unsympathetic state governments took their toll. The once rich and proud lines found cannibalization (sale of assets) as a short term solution. Longer term, it appeared that only a merger might create the possibility of another one hundred years of prosperity.

The Penn Central merger was built on a foundation of hope. Hope that merger would equate with streamlined plant and elimination of overlapping branches fighting for too few carloads. Hope that merger would permit better utilization of locomotives, cars, personnel, and equipment. Hope that a new corporation would possess the ability to negotiate modern work rules with labor and eliminate "full crew" laws. And perhaps, above all, hope that merger of these two behemoths would create a corporation of sufficient clout in Washington D.C. to ameliorate both the passenger problem and the obdurate attitude of the freight rate-making bureaucracy of the ICC.

Some will say there was one more hope; hope that the assets of the railroads could be parleyed into more profitable enterprise and that this diversification into business with more respectable rates of return would improve the overall corporate bottom line. Would this sap the strength of the railroad by draining capital away from much needed improvements? Perhaps. Over twenty years later railroads still diversify, and the debate still rages.

There is no debate, however, that once created on

---

*All references in this book to "Penn Central" or "PC" refer to the various names of the Penn Central Company's Railroad during 1968 - 1976. Technically, it was Pennsylvania New York Central Transportation Company 2/1/68 - 5/8/68; Penn Central Company 5/8/68 - 10/1/69; Penn Central Transportation Company 10/1/69 to 4/1/76. PCT Company filed for bankruptcy 6/21/70, followed by parent holding company, Penn Central. Most assets of PCT were conveyed to Conrail 4/1/76, while the holding company reorganized and still exists (1987).

that February morn in 1968, the going got even tougher for the newly combined lines. That very first year of merger resulted in substantial losses for the rail unit of Penn Central. Shippers started to grumble as service which had enjoyed traditional routings for many years was subjected to major delays as cars ended up on the "other line's" side of town, or got lost in incompatible computer systems. Derailments rose to unprecedented levels as deferred maintenance took its toll, and talented executives took to the doors when departments were meshed and the two lines were found to have fundamentally different operating and marketing procedures.

Dark clouds were gathering on the horizon as Penn Central bade farewell to its merger year. Apparently the ICC did not see the new railroad as a sickly newborn, but as a giant capable of herculean feats. On January 1, 1969 it gave PC its Augean stable — the perpetually moribund New York, New Haven and Hartford Railroad. New Haven in the 1960's was an anachronism from the 1920's trying valiantly to save its already bankrupt life. With its New England manufacturing base emasculated, NH would have done well to simply break even on its meager freight operations. Coupled to this unfirm foundation, however, was a large money losing passenger operation. In 1968, PC had handled over 36 million commuters. With New Havens inclusion in 1969, this figure jumped to 54 million a year. Hardly a growth business.

And things got worse. The post office department continued a policy of diverting mail and parcel post away from the rails and onto trucks and planes. The terms "Red team" and "Green team" came into our vocabulary as PC personnel from the Headquarters to the Yard Offices refused to work as a "Penn Central" team. The actual costs of integrating the rail systems was proving far in excess of estimates and many anticipated savings were simply not drawn down to the bottom line. A lack of equipment in good working order sent the per diem (car hire) debit skyrocketing. As usual the ICC continued to react with dinosaurian slowness in response to PC requests for freight increases. Labor continued to win increases which were not balanced with increased revenues. In addition, a general business slump affecting the entire nation, was keenly felt by a Penn Central which was created on the predication that the economy would expand. Another new term, "Stagflation," (inflation within a recession) was coined and had dire consequences for the new firm. From a high of $71 Penn Central stock sank to under $30 by the end of 1969 as some Wall Streeters began to perceive that perhaps something was fundamentally wrong with the Company that had inherited the record of the longest consecutive common dividend (122 years) in American history. Some were unshaken till the end. In 1969 Penn Central would lose hundreds of millions on its' rail operation.

1970 arrived with a snowstorm that would paralyze the already gasping colossus. Infighting at the very top of PC management and pressure by the lending banks had resulted in a new president. Nonrail investments were turning spectacularly sour. Top

management frightened away any would-be help from the financial community by tales of conflicts of interest, "creative accounting" and "insider selling" of stock by Penn Central Board Members. In the first *quarter* of 1970 PC would report a loss of over 100 million on its rail operations! The Company was on the ropes awaiting a final knockdown.

Almost mercifully, it came on June 21, 1970. Desperate for an infusion of cash, the Company had found all doors on Wall Street and in Washington closed. The merger built on hope had not even lasted 1000 days (872 to be exact). The likes of Commodore Vanderbilt or a J. Edgar Thompson would be replaced by court appointed trustees. Out on the high iron, the trains continued to run under Section 77 of the Bankruptcy Act, but the railroad would never be the same.

Penn Central would be better known as a bankrupt railroad (almost 6 years) as compared to its 2 plus years of "solvency." The trustees attempted many innovative ideas to stabilize the road and place it in position for a Plan of Reorganization. Most of the fundamental changes they longed for, however, were simply reiterations of solutions that had been identified and rejected in the past. Relief from archaic labor provisions and governmental rate making was just not forthcoming. Permission to reduce the railroad to a 15,000 mile "core" never materialized. States still insisted on operation of commuter trains and seldom used branches without fully compensating the Company for its endeavors. The establishment of Amtrak on May 1, 1971 and greater involvement by State Commuter Authorities helped but couldn't fully stop the losses on the passenger side. In June of '72 a "tropical storm" named "Agnes" devasted the northeast and inflicted over 40 million in damages to Penn Central. Freight carloads nosedived in late '74 and into

1975 and throughout all the bankrupt years the roadbed continued to deteriorate badly as the rehabilitation projections for PC were reaching into the billions. Although gradually tightened up, the freights continued their operations much as before and new ideas like "Ship-A-Train" (high volume shipments of piggyback trailers) were simply not radical enough to get PC back on firm footing.

Operating 65% of Amtrak's passenger services, most of the nation's commuter trains, and 19,000 miles of freight trackage the government knew it could not let PC's operations grind to a halt. Finally, faced with the realization that no management could make Penn Central work under the current rules of the game, Congress approved and President Gerry Ford signed the Railroad Revitalization and Regulatory Reform Act of 1976. This 4-R Act would be the basis for what President Ford called "the first significant reform of transportation regulation . . . in more than 25 years." 4-R set the tone which allowed Penn Central and several other bankrupt eastern railroads to be reborn again under the aegis of the Consolidated Railroad Company (Conrail). Relieved of the Northeast Corridor passenger operations (to Amtrak), relieved of commuter train operations (to the recipient states), relieved of thousands of excess employees (to government funded retirement), Conrail took the throttle from Penn Central's hands on April 1, 1976. Endowed with the ability to adjust its freight rates to the market, to more easily rid itself of inefficient branchlines and facilities, Conrail was able to take the core of the former Penn Central and within a few years put it solidly in "the black" for years to come. One can only wonder if the 4-R Act had been signed in February 1968 instead of February 1975, would Penn Central have come to the same end?

Penn Central Motive Power Chronicle

In order to develop an appreciation of the motive power of the Penn Central Railroad one must be acquainted with the locomotives of the Company's procreators. In the early morning of February 1, 1968, Pennsy and Central locked knuckles in the staid halls of the Philadlephia and New York City headquarters of the new Company. It would take weeks, even months, however, before this change would be felt on the head end of the trains. The railroad was operating in February just as it had done in January, with New York Central and Pennsylvania engines toiling at the same tasks they always did but now technically with the word "former" in front of their name. Although new locomotives would soon infiltrate this vast fleet, Penn Central's motive power origins were 100% NYC, PRR, and NYNH&H. Let us examine how these ancestors developed the diesel and electric locomotive rosters they mustered for Penn Central at its embarkation.

After extensive unproductive tests with duplex drives and turbines, and hastened by that red ink Centennial Year of 1946, the Pennsylvania Railroad turned to diesels with a vengeance in the late 1940's. Buying literally almost every diesel offered in the builder's catalog (and with Baldwin's cooperation, even creating some new ones), the PRR saw diesels as a major cost reducer in this post war inflationary period. By the early 1950's, the PRR's road fleet was principally composed of the 1500-1600 horsepower

cab units of all four builders (EMD, Alco-GE, Baldwin, and Fairbanks Morse). The sidelines and yards were patrolled by just about every conceivable hood or switcher unit built. In fact, in describing the early PRR diesel fleet it is less effort to simply enumerate the major classes of diesels they somehow missed . . . namely, FT, F2, BL2, E1- E6, and the DL-109.

New York Central fared no better early on in the diesel buying game. After also sampling just about all of each builders' wares, the Central settled down to running its mainlines primarily with large fleets of F7's and FA's on the freights and E7's and 8's on the passenger trains. The small accumulations of Baldwin and FM cabs were quickly corraled onto secondary runs, while an impressive array of GP7's and RS3's proved well suited to their General Purpose billing. Like the PRR, NYC also managed to purchase almost every switcher offered by the several builders.

Ever the Alco loyalist in the days of steam, New Haven acquired quite a respectable tally of diesels from that builder. Having successfully employed the versatile DL-109 during the War, when peace came to the land, New Haven completed its diesel development with liberal doses of Alco-GE FA cabs, and several issues of Alco switchers and road switchers. Add in a small pocket of FM power (C-Liners and early H16-44's), and New Haven was able to polish off steam operations by 1951, among the first in the nation (and notably, without any help from General Motors).

To best describe the profusion of diesels purchased by these three Penn Central parents, it could be suggested that if a "Diesel Spotter's Guide" were to be penned during this period, it could be illustrated with photos of only PRR, NYC and NH diesels and have very few significant omissions.

Meanwhile, during the early to mid fifties, steam continued to puff away on the Pennsylvania and New

York Central Railroads. Traffic surges and slumps brought total dieselization tauntingly close on several occasions, but it was not until 1957 that the last fires burned down on both lines as steady infusions of GP9's finally delivered the merciful finishing blow. With the urgency of elimination of steam engines and their facilities out of the way, all three roads turned their attention to standardization and upgrading of their diesel fleets. Intermediate programs of this were

begun in the mid to late fifties, since the complete rebuilding programs later introduced by the manufacturers were not yet in full swing.

New York Central, unhappy with the high maintenance costs and relative unreliability of their Baldwin, FM and Lima fleets, tried installing EMD 567's in their carbodies, while the PRR experimented by having Alco rebuild several Baldwin Sharks. Neither road was entirely satisfied with its efforts. New Haven was faced with a more immediate problem since its roster was comparatively older, chiefly due to its reliance on the 60 DL109's dating from the early 1940's and a seriously outmoded electric locomotive stable. New Haven's solution to this problem was the scrapping of those locomotives and the acquisition of brand new Alco RS11's, FM H16-44's and their first taste of EMD power: GP9's, SW1200's and unique FL9's. A small FA and RS3 rebuilding program by Alco rounded out this NH improvement project.

Electric locomotives historically last a long time and the three Penn Central predecessors played a large part in the creation of that maxim. By the 1950's the future partners were operating electric locomotives which were 20-30 years of age and while turning in very commendable performances, the day was not too far distant when replacement would be necessary. Early in the fifties, New Haven took delivery of 10 EP-5 rectifiers for passenger service and replaced the remainder of its aging electric roster with pseudo-electric FL9's several years later. Happily, they also purchased some nearly new (in electric locomotive terms) E33 rectifiers from the Norfolk & Western (ex Virginian).

Pennsy, seemingly always ultra-conservative in its electric locomotive development began to explore for a successor to its substantial P5 electric fleet which had been plying the rails since electrification of the mainlines in the 1930's. First attempts were made in the early fifties by sampling state of the art experiments by Baldwin - Westinghouse and General Electric. By 1959 the nod was given to General Electric to replace the experimentals, all the P5's and a few oddballs with a fleet of 65 4400 horsepower E44 rectifiers. Passenger service remained undisturbed when it was deemed the peerless GG-1 could continue for the immediate future.

Only New York Central seemed content to do

little in the electric locomotive field. With no pressing freight electric demands, and with passenger operations on the wane, NYC chose only to continually shuffle the best engines to the forefront; for instance, when the isolated Cleveland electric island was dieselized, the many wheeled CUT P2 locomotives were sent to the Hudson Division. By about 1961 electric operations on all three roads stabilized and remained virtually intact until the PC nuptials of '68 and '69.

As the new decade arrived, Pennsy and the Central were becoming increasingly aware that their diesel fleets could be vastly upgraded through procurement of locomotives developed in a new era of dieseldom. . . the "second generation" of diesels. New York Central opened the door early in 1961 by purchasing small trial orders of 15 EMD GP20's and 15 Alco DL721's. The low nose GP20's were sufficiently promising for NYC to come back for more small orders of 10 GP30's and 31 GP35's in the next years. Alco, however, was completely displaced by its former partner General Electric whose 2500 hp U25B was ordered and reordered by NYC. The PRR also found the U25B an excellent engine and gave GE orders for 59 units from 1962-1965. By this time, though, the PRR was following the national tide and turning more and more towards EMD. In 1963 an order for 52 GP30's was followed during the next two years with successive orders for 59 and 60 2500 hp GP35's. On both NYC and PRR these early second generation orders were used to clear the attics of some of the most inefficient, old or oddball units, cleansing the rosters of units most dear to railfans hearts. . . Centipedes, PA's, FT's, Erie Builts, C-Liners, etc. New Haven, initially sated by its late '50's locomotive program and beset by greater financial problems, finally ordered some Century 425's and U25B's in 1964 (significantly, reinstituting its old policy of snubbing EMD). One year later another order for the popular U25B would end New Haven's contribution to the pool of diesels that Penn Central would inherit.

The year 1965 initiated an interesting shift in motive power policies. While both PRR and NYC seemed pleased by their U25B and GP35 orders, NYC veered away by shunning the Alcos and C-C hoods that rival PRR began to buy. On line builder Alco was no doubt embarrassed by the absence of orders from

the Central for its new Century series. Pennsy still stuck with Alco, however, buying Century 425's and ordering 15 of the new six axle Century 628. The C628 order along with an order for 40 SD35's and 20 U25C's began a significant divergence in diesel preferences between the future partners.

1966 was a year of major changes in the whole of dieseldom and especially in regard to the Pennsy

and Central. Fueled by a railroad industry flush with the first respectable profits produced in some time, the builders got down to the trade-in business in earnest. Both EMD and GE began production of new lines of diesels with important improvements and Alco, already third man out, saw its very survival in doubt as it fell even further behind the pack. EMD introduced its new 645 engine series (GP40, SD40, SD45) early in the year, and GE upped the horsepower on its U series at first to 2800 hp and then to 3000. Both builders, perhaps unknowingly, also changed the face of the diesel world that year from one of new carbody styles concurrent with every new model, to standardized carbodies for succeeding models. The carbodies sculpted for the GP40 and U28B would remain essentially the same over the next twenty years even though meaningful changes were taking place under the skin

with each model change. Both Pennsy and Central would take up these changed diesels rather quickly. It was necessary in order to handle the increasing traffic, but also because the diesels they were operating were mostly acquired in the steam to diesel rush of 1948-52; consequently they were now over 15 years old and due for major rebuilding or replacement. The cab units of the lesser builders had been easy targets in the early sixties, but now it was time to turn to the F7's, RS3's, FA's, and non EMD hoods. As this effort began on the

two railroads, the diesel preferences that had surfaced in 1965, became obvious in 1966, and would accelerate for the next two years before the merger.

Water level NYC would assemble an imposing fleet of 58 U30B's and 105 GP40's in 1966 and '67. This was in line with the image it had of itself; an efficient, fast carrier of profitable merchandise traffic . . . auto racks, hot slab steel, Flexi Van, Flexi Flo. On the other hand, PRR would not order a single GP40 or U30B. Now shunning the B-B (4 axle) entirely, Pennsy continued to favor the C-C (6 axle) for its mountainous terrain and substantial mineral traffic by placing orders for 30 Century 630- 636's, 40 U28-30-33C's, and 65 SD40's during this period. Penn did modify this divergence, however, by accepting EMD advertisements of ". . . a locomotive that can run like a race horse and drag like a mule" . . . the 3600 hp SD45. PRR ordered 130 of these 20 cylindered beasts after 1966. And finally, for some unknown, perhaps benevolent reason, NYC ordered 10 Century 430's from Alco just before the merger. Ironically, this nearly final production run of Alco would become the last new locomotives delivered to the New York Central (December '67) before the Penn Central union. (The last PRR locomotives delivered were SD45's in January '68). In summary, Pennsy contributed 2181 diesel and electric locomotives to the Penn Central roster; New York Central 1799.

On February 1, 1968 the author was enroute from Philadelphia to Newark, N.J. aboard a nameless passenger train. Trackside, nothing appeared any different. It was just another dreary winter day in the northeast. The coach was the usual P70 and up front a GG1 hummed along as they had done so well for so many years. At home that night, however, the "tube" would announce the apocalyptic news of the merger. As the announcer droned on, the background tape showed the world our first glimpse of a "Penn Central" diesel. Less than impressive is probably the only kind way to describe the newly painted SD40 slowly rolling by officials at Philadelphia, Pa. Apprehensively, we pondered not only the stark modernistic paint scheme but also the loss of two old friends.

The Penn Central choice for a paint scheme was unfortunate and perhaps even foreboding. It would come to empathically symbolize the later tragedies of that Company. The utilitarian pigment was understandable since both NYC and PRR also had had black as a base color for their freight units since their very first diesel purchases some 30 years earlier. Both Pennsy and Central, however, had used some classic, colored striping and red keystones or ovals to highlight and employ the black as a foil. Of course passenger units deserved a tasteful Tuscan red or gray paint scheme; a rolling advertisement for the corporation. None of this "class" was apparent in this new Penn Central paint design. Apparently the railfans were not the only ones disappointed, since soon after, PC started experimenting with red "P's" or orange "C's," to modify the pattern. After a few half-hearted attempts, however, the two white letters P and C intwined (the worms in love) became standard, to the almost universal scorn of the trackside.

As with all mergers, Penn Central initially found itself short of motive power and quickly availed itself of the locomotives on the current lease markets (the ubiquitous B&LE F7's and DM&IR SD9's to name a few). Many a Baldwin or Alco switcher got a short reprieve on life during this period while GP7's and 9's happily took to the road freights again. Some minimal preparation for the merger had taken place in '66 when both fleets were renumbered into like groups as well as to avoid conflicting numbers. NYC had even started ordering new diesels with dynamic brakes, but most expensive on board modifications to existing diesels (e.g. cab signaling) had not yet taken place. Generally speaking, during the first months of the merger PRR units would be used as B or trailing units on NYC mainlines and vice versa.

Although new locomotives in Penn Central garb started arriving almost immediately after the merger date (e.g. 20 U33C's ordered by PRR were arriving in PC paint just weeks after the merger), Penn Central itself did not order any new engines until several months into the merger. Then the purchases seemed to be almost a perfect blending of PRR and NYC past practices, as orders for 100 units were divided up among GP40, SD45, U33B, and U33C models.

Dragged kicking and screaming to the altar on January 1, 1969 Penn Central found itself in a shotgun marriage to the bankrupt New Haven Railroad. Heavy in passenger operations, light in freight, fighting for its corporate existence for years, Penn Central found little in New Haven's motive power dowry that could mesh well into the larger company's freight system. Aside from the GP9's, FL9's, Century

425's, U25B's, and E33's the addition of the New Haven operations would place yet another drain on the PC pool of power. As PC infused ex PRR E8's, RS3's, and GG1's into the New Haven Region, trackside one could witness a parade of derelict ex NH units in various states of cannibalization heading west toward the scrap heap as PC cleaned out the NH boneyards in Boston and Cedar Hill. The New Haven Railroad in

summation contributed a total of 316 diesels and electrics to PC.

In its last full solvent year of 1969, Penn Central found the monies to order still more locomotives but shopped with a somewhat less flashy bent. The order for 150 GP38's was meaningful not only as a new model for Penn Central, but in that it represented the compromise unit that could truly find universal system use. Also in '69 PC finally gave some attention to its switchers by instituting a program to rebuild 60

EMD switchers and equip them with MU capabilities, larger fuel tanks and roller bearings. This slant towards less "glamorous," intermediate horsepower diesels accelerated the next year as PC chose to purchase more units for the sidelines and yards when orders for SW1500's, SD38's and U23C's were effected. The orders for these new models helped spell the end for PC's last remaining FM units which had been centralized in Chicago.

Bankrupt on June 21, 1970, Penn Central found the purpose of its existence changed radically. Shock, dismay, anger, sickness . . . choose one or all of those words to describe the reaction of railfan and railroader alike. Almost immediately, it seemed, Penn Central started to show a new raggedness in the appearance of its motive power. Later as new management arrived and tales of "Red team," "Green team" were bandied about, the order was put out in early 1971 to "Penn Centralize" all power as it came in for monthlies and the like. Power began to show up with the former owner's name and herald hurriedly blacked out and replaced by a PC worm. Some units were almost completely bald except for the number and a single small worm on the nose of the unit. Full paint jobs seemed to be the last thing on management's mind during this period and hundreds of diesels would never receive anything more than this "temporary, interim" work (indeed, hundreds of units arrived 4/1/76 on Conrail's doorstep in PRR Brunswick green or NYC black!)

Penn Central motive power policies now began to settle down while the much larger game of corporate survival was played out. Still in need of reliable locomotives, PC turned solidly in favor of the 2000-2300 hp non-turbocharged road switchers (GP38, GP38-2, and U23B). In the years following bankruptcy, PC would accumulate a virtual armada of (almost 500) GP38's and its improved successor the GP38-2. As the Shark would symbolize the Pennsy, the FL9 the New Haven, and probably the FA the Central, the GP38 represents the Penn Central. It could be found systemwide in just about any conceivable mainline, branch, yard or transfer service. The PC GP38 was a "clergyman's special" of a locomotive: no frills, no extras, easy on the gas and repairs, but good dependable transportation. Hand in hand with their gradual acquisition came the demise of almost all the remaining Baldwin road switchers and switchers. Penn Central would enter Conrail with a pure EMD, GE and Alco roster (except for a mere 3 Baldwins). To the 4296 locomotives it had inherited from its predecessors, Penn Central had added a total of 938 more.

On April 1, 1976, the Consolidated Railroad Company relieved Penn Central of its railroad operations. The PC fleet formed the basis into which the motive power of the other components of Conrail was blended. Some PC locomotives kept their black paint and "worms" for several years while Conrail took hold. Perhaps due to the fact that the Conrail numbering system for its locomotives was built around the PC system, Penn Central engines seemed to survive in a "pure state" somewhat longer than their EL, LV, CNJ, and RDG brethren. Conrail was soon on profitable footing however, and began a systematic program of replacing all of its inherited power with diesels of the third generation. By the late 1980's only some GP38's, GP38-2's, U23B's, U23C's, SD38's, SW1500's, SD40's, GP40's and some rebuilt EMD switchers remained of the huge Penn Central fleet of diesels. In numerical sequence, let us look at that roster at work and at rest.

1000 Series: Freight Cab Units

FA 1
1009-1333*

The FA1 was a 1500 hp freight cab unit built by Alco-GE after WWII until October '50. The three NYC FA1's were never re-painted Penn Central and by the end of 1968 were in scraplines. As 1969 arrived, however, PC once again found itself operating FA1's when it inherited NH's four. These units, originally numbered 0401, 0418, 0426, and 0428, were quickly renumbered 1330 - 1333 and remained at work in the Boston area. Their duties in this populous area, and relative celebrity status made them the Penn Central FA's fans are most familiar with. 1330 is shown in full PC regalia (above) at Boston, May 18, 1969. 1333

(below) however, has a simpler scheme atop its New Haven paint at Dover Street, Boston, July 1970.

* Roster numbers given in this location on the photo pages should be considered only guidelines. In some cases, there *may* be gaps in the numbering or even completely different model types within the "guideline" numbers given. For more precise identification, see Roster on pages 230-241. Logos here will designate originating railroads of model class.

Herbert H. Harwood

(Right) The angle of a FA windshield proved to be too tempting a target to rock throwing urchins on overhead bridges in the Boston environs, so Penn Central erected steel mesh grills over this FA1's glass (the same FA seen one month earlier, opposite page).

(Below) BL-1 (Boston - Lowell) is underway through Readville, Massachusetts. At this time, July 1969, this was the last area in America to find a perfect A-B-B-A Alco Cab combination.

M.S. Zak Collection

E. D. Galvin, Herbert H. Harwood Collection

J. W. Swanberg

(Left) By the fall of 1972, the FA era on the Penn Central was over. The New Haven units were traded into General Electric and the last FA, ex NYC 1302, an FA2, sat awaiting an uncertain fate in the deadline at Altoona on September 17, 1972. It and FA1 1333 were fortunate to be saved for use as cab cars on LIRR commuter trains.

FA2
1044-1399

The "flatnosed" FA2 was an Alco-GE product from late 1950 until the mid-fifties. While PRR had retired all of its 24 FA2's at least a year before merger time, exactly 1/2 of NYC's impressive fleet of 88, still in their original 1000 and 1100 numbers, remained.

(Right, top) One month after the February 1, 1968 merger FA2 1089 rests in the engine terminal at Weehawken, N.J. next to a paint scheme it would never bear.

R. J. Yanosey

(Center) Shortly later, Penn Central set out to renumber the FA's by adding 300 to the NYC numbers, such as the 1398 formerly NYC 1098 at Collinwood, Ohio on August 4, 1968.

M. S. Zak Collection

(Below) The emblems may read Pennsylvania and New York Central, but these 2 freight cabs are the property of the Penn Central Company. PRR F7 1503 and NYC FA2 1389, (the former 1089 in the top photo), swap stories at Detroit, Michigan in October 1968. Oddly, both horns face forward on 1389.

J. W. Swanberg.

William J. Brennan

(Above) "Messerschmidts": that's what some NYC engineers called the FA's that their road stabled. By 1968, however, they were not descending on cities with symbol trains along the mainline at top track speed; instead they were relegated to secondary runs, like this local working at the yard in Croton, N.Y., April 1968.

(Below) "Getting out of town" and into third rail territory, these FA's sport two slightly different paint schemes and sandwich an interesting phenomenon: a hood unit from the same builder that is about a year and a half older, RS2 5229.

William J. Brennan

Herbert H. Harwood

M.S. Zak, RJY Collection

F7
1440-1906

The familiar "Bulldog" face of the 1500 hp EMD F7 was the predominant freight road diesel of the early 1950's. Built from Feb. '49 till Dec. '53 the F7 was extremely popular with both PRR and NYC and hundreds were ordered. While certainly not unscathed, the F7 fleets of both roads had survived the "trade in" fever of the sixties better than the freight cabs of any other builder. Many would, in fact, continue to give good service throughout PC's entire history, although the ex PRR units were just about gone by Conrail's inception. Interesting lashups of these PRR and NYC F7's would occur in the early days of the merger; for example, this ABA set (above) at Baltimore in 2/69.

Some of the ex PRR F7's in the 1400 series began life as F3's geared for helper service on the Allegheny slopes. Rebuilt to F7 specs and regeared by PRR in the fifties, they enjoyed a short span of service on Penn Central, as did 1455 (center). Despite the reworking, similar 1457, (below), is back to her

original haunts, shoving on the rear of trains "on the hill." Shown at Cresson, Pa. just before the merger in May 1967, 1457 still sports F3 style numberboards. PC also operated several unrepainted "pure" ex PRR F3's in this carbody early in the merger. The several "chicken wire" F3's that did survive into Penn Central included one PRR and four NYC A units; none lasted more than a few months and none would see any PC markings beyond the number.

R.J. Yanosey

RJY Collection

R.J. Yanosey

(Above) The ancestry of PC 1482 shows clearly in this shot of the F7A at Blue Island, Ill., January 1971.

(Left) To 1501 belongs the dubious distinction of being the last of the PRR F7's, actually seeing several months of Conrail service. The lift rings on the nose are the quick clue to ex PRR cab units in Penn Central paint. 1501, formerly PRR 9801A, was at Collinwood, Ohio in October of 1976.

(Below) PC 1659 is in the lead of a lashup composed of 5 F7 and FA A&B units, all of which were previously owned by New York Central. Their train is eastbound through Berea, Ohio on the ex NYC mainline in August 1968. 1659 originally had a stream-lined coupler covering, such as the E units once wore, to protect the engine crew from the impaling effect a knuckle had on an auto or truck struck on a grade crossing. It was felt the covering would enable the stricken vehicle to "bounce off" rather than be scraped down the tracks for a half a mile with a knuckle coupler impaled through the front door. By this time in its life, however, 1659 has long had the covering removed, coupler welded straight and all that remains is the nonstandard pilot.

W.T. Stuart, Herbert H. Harwood Collection

21

(Right) PC 1707 has weathered well in the 15 months since her portrait was taken in fresh paint in May 1968 as shown in the color photo on page 130. Here she rests between assignments at New Castle, Pa. on August 14, 1969, a remembrance to the short lived "red P" experiments. Perhaps later that day 1707 helped haul some of New Castle's clay products to market or further some P&LE or B&O interchange traffic.

(Center, below) Sister 1735, still in her native NYC livery, forms another interesting "all in the family" lashup at Baltimore almost one year earlier.

(Bottom) Out at Enola, PC 1747 wears the ultimate in simple paint schemes as she and sister 1727, coupled together "elephant style," start a westbound out of the yard. This is September 5, 1970 and if you watch carefully in succeeding pictures, you will be able to follow the construction progress of Interstate 81 in the background. Incidently, the track at the left where that caboose with the interesting PC paint job sits is called the "pimple." Its purpose is to give that caboose a little altitude so that

once the end of that freight clears, the switches at the bottom of the "pimple" can be thrown and the caboose can roll down and couple to the rear.

Herbert H. Harwood

(Right) PC 1758 displays the paint scheme most Penn Central F7's wore (or were supposed to wear anyway). Altoona, Pa. August 1976.

(Center) 1780 teams up with a GP35 from one time rival Pennsy to haul tonnage eastbound through the bridge over the Maumee River in Toledo, Ohio in May 1968. During these early months NYC units often led on ex NYC trackage for cab signal reasons and because the PRR units lacked "Agreement" seats for the engineers. These cushioned seats and armrests were to be installed on all units by August 1, 1968. When the deadline wasn't met a strike was threatened but did not materialize. The extensive Traffic Control (TCS) work done by the NYC in the fifties and sixties is apparent in this photo of the freight headed east on the "wrong main."

(Bottom) A F7-FP7-F7 combo takes a "Yard Puller" (transfer between various Cleveland area yards) westbound at Puritas Road, Cleveland, September, 1976.

R.J.Yanosey

R.J.Yanosey

Herbert H. Harwood

23

(Right) In addition to her sporty "red P" paint job, PC 1839 has had her portholes removed and replaced with sheet metal. Idling in the hot summer sun, she sits with sisters still in their NYC paint at Detroit, July 11, 1968.

(Below) As happens in all mergers initially, power pools often get disturbed, and diesels often find themselves far from home. Such was the case just after Conrail was created, and thus we see PC 1853 and three brethren far away from their Collinwood haunts and on the tracks of the former Lehigh Valley Railroad at West Oak Island, Newark, N.J., July 1976. While the engines might read Penn Central, and the train is Conrail's, the crew is ex LV. While boarding the F7 at Oak Island engine terminal the rather rotund engineer was heard to curse the F7 and its high side steps, grumbling that the Valley had had this type and had scrapped them "years ago."

J.W. Swanberg

R.J. Yanosey

One month after the merger, ex NYC 1864 wears a new coat of black as night approaches at Weehawken. Once regular inhabitants of the West Shore route down the Hudson River, the F7's would soon leave to congregate in the midwest.

R.J. Yanosey

M.S. Zak Collection

Far away from its home PC 1878 belies her true origins under her black paint. Seeking trade in value, Penn Central purchased a group of supposedly obsolete F7's from the Rio Grande (D&RGW RR). The PC mechanical people inspecting them found 4 units, 2 A's and 2 B's, that were in as good a mechanical shape as anything PC was operating at the time. In true phoenix fashion, the veteran cabs were sent east to join PC's F7 pool in Collinwood. Initially the 5700 series Rio Grande units had the front "5" taken off their number and were hurridly put to work with nothing more than the western road's name painted out and a white PC worm (page 132). By November 12, 1973 when this photo was taken, however, the western diesels had been painted black and assigned PC F7 series numbers in the 1870's (A's) and 3400's (B's). The lucky westerners would persist well into Conrail.

M.S. Zak Collection

PC 1905 idles next to a fellow Pennsylvania Railroad locomotive at Conway Yards in August 1968. The 4 ex PRR F7's renumbered into the low 1900's and tacked onto the end of the NYC F7's were special "merger" units equipped in 1966 with both PRR cab signals and NYC ATS equipment, making them capable of leading in either PRR or NYC territory. Some GP35's and U25B's from both roads were similarly modified.

25

2000 Series: High Horsepower Roadswitchers

All - M. S. Zak Collection

GP38
2010-2014

The five GP38's in the 2000 series were ordered for the Pennsylvania Reading Seashore Lines, a New Jersey railroad owned by Penn Central and the Reading Company. Three months after their August 1970 order date, they emerged from the Electro Motive Division in fresh PRSL paint to be "set up" for the trip east. Within a week, however, all five were reported to have had their PRSL heralds painted out and PC worms applied on the nose. Apparently, the financial credit of PRSL was now suspect in the months following the bankruptcy. An accommodation was quickly made whereby parent PC, bankrupt but more credit worthy than little PRSL, was allowed to assume "ownership" of the orphaned units. Ironically the PC'd diesels were assigned to work in the area around the PRSL and often were seen in the PRSL's Camden, N.J. facilities, while the "poor" PRSL was forced to keep some Baldwins it had sought to retire, running for a few more years.

2014 illustrates a perfectly illuminated roster shot at the Camden engine terminal February 14, 1971 (left top).

2010 bearing a PC herald on the long hood, had taken a transfer up to Morrisville, Pa. on January 31, 1971 (middle).

Several years later (2/11/73), PC 2013 takes a freight east out of Camden's Pavonia Yard (below).

DL721

2021 - 2044

NEW YORK
CENTRAL
SYSTEM

M.S. Zak Collection

In 1960, responding to EMD's newly introduced 2000 hp GP20, Alco revamped its 1800 hp Dl701 (RS11) and started advertising the 2000 hp DL721 or RS32. Equipped with a 251 V12 turbocharged engine the new locomotive was an improvement over previous Alco's, but was not well received. Out distanced by new GP30 and U25B competition, the DL721's record foretold of the upcoming decade which would find most railroads abandoning Alco on the second round of diesel sales. Only Southern Pacific and New York Central would order the unit and then only to the tune of 35 units. NYC tried to be loyal to on-line Alco, by ordering fifteen of the units in June 1961 and ten more a year later, but the DL721 model would prove to be the last new Alco purchased by the Central for a long six years.

(Top) PC 2029 started life as NYC 8029, then was renumbered in 1966 to NYC 2029. A unit which once could be found at the head end of fast NYC "SV" trains now is but a switcher at New Castle, Pa., March 9, 1969.

R.J. Yanosey

R.J. Yanosey and William J. Brennan

(Center) In fresh PC black, 2027 locks knuckles at Weehawken, N.J. with one of the GP30's which caused its relative scarcity. It's still early in the merger, October 1968, and many transfers between ex PRR and ex NYC facilities are necessary. This one, Extra 2027 West, will depart this former NYC yard, traverse the National Docks Branch (ex NYC), up a new PC built connection to the Passaic & Harsimus Branch (ex PRR), and arrive in the former PRR Meadows Yard.

(Left) After a few years of service on the hottest mainline trains the NYC ran, the DL721's were relegated to secondary "plugs" for NYC and PC. Here is 2043 southbound with a local at Cold Spring, N.Y. in June 1968. Still in Central paint here, the Alco would endure until early 1979, when Conrail traded it to General Electric. Fortunately, however, a last minute reprieve from the scrapper arrived, as it and nine comrades were resold to the Chicago & Northwestern. They served out their days as heavy switchers and local freight power in the Upper Penninsula of Michigan, before the metal shredder finally caught up with them in 1986.

R.J. Yanosey

C430
2050 - 2059

R.J. Yanosey

After the orders for the 25 DL721's in '61 and '62, the New York Central resisted all of the new Alco models until several months before the PC merger. Aware that the historic builder was literally on the verge of folding up, NYC along with some other roads that had not ordered Alco's for many years (notably UP and C&O), finally found it in their corporate hearts to give Alco some token orders for Centuries. In line with its high horsepower B-B policy, NYC chose 10 Century 430's which were delivered in December 1967 just before the merger. The units, equipped with new high adhesion trucks, were good but simply couldn't find a niche on a road so heavily into standardization (read GE and GM). After perhaps a year or two in general mainline service, the Centuries were placed in a pool serving the well known Weirton-Mingo Junction steel area. Most were sought out and photographed in this service as Alco's became scarcer in the seventies, such as 2055 at Mingo Jct in October 1976 (left). The big Alcos served out their days in Mingo to Cleveland service and most were sold in the early eighties to two NJ roads, the Morristown & Erie and the New York Susquehanna & Western. (2055, for instance was sold to NYS&W where it became that road's #3008).

2052 (above) and friends uncouple from an eastbound autorack train in Weehawken two months after the merger when the unit was still entrusted with hotshot mainline business. The background is interesting, not only for the ventilation buildings of the Lincoln Tunnel, but because of the cliffs in back of them. Atop these cliffs on July 11, 1804, Aaron Burr killed Alexander Hamilton in a gun duel. It really wasn't much of a fight since Hamilton refused to fire, not wishing to injure Burr. Mr. Burr was not so gallant, however, and shot the Secretary of the Treasury, who died the next day. Burr would live on for another thirty years, politically and emotionally dead.

M.S. Zak Collection

R.J. Yanosey

R.J. Yanosey

GP20
2100 - 2112

Faced with dwindling sales after the steam to diesel feasts of the 1940's and 50's, EMD was obligated to find a superior product for the dieselized U.S. railroads. The first real attempt at this began production late in 1959 emerging as the turbocharged 2000 hp GP20. This unit incorporated many improvements while still keeping the basic 567 engine common to thousands of other EMD's already on the rails. The logic of three modern 2000 hp GP20's replacing 4 antiquated 1500 hp cab units seemed inescapable, and the GP20 started a wave which would change the face of dieseldom once again.

(Top) PC 2105 at Youngstown, Ohio 5/20/69 illustrates the GP20 as built. Of Penn Central's three predecessors, only NYC purchased this model.

(Center) By 1972, Penn Central was enjoying the economies of more modern diesels (GP38's) which could produce 2000 hp without that super costly turbocharger. The Company began to perform "turbo lobotomies" on some of the GP20's such as 2103 at Selkirk, N.Y., October 1973, upgrading the unit with 645 engine parts and paper air filters in the process.

(Below) Four years earlier, in May of 1968, however, GP20's were still mainline power and the same 2103, in unrebuilt "pure" form leads a mixed lashup westward across the Maumee River in Toledo, Ohio.

(NEXT PAGE) Also in May 1968. 2109 starts an equally interesting lashup up the River Line and out of the tunnel from Weehawken at North Bergen, N.J. (R.J. Yanosey).

D. Hamley, RJY Collection

GP30
2188 - 2249

The GP30 was the 2250 hp improvement of the GP20 introduced by EMD in mid 1961. Unmistakable, with its bulging dynamic brake blister "shoulders" showing GMC truck influence, the GP30 was the first nationally accepted EMD second generation model.

While NYC purchased only 10, like 2193 (above) at Conway, Pa. and 2188 (right) at Weehawken in September 1968, Pennsy used the GP30 as its first major entrant into the second generation when it ordered 52 of the muscular hoods, such as 2212 (below) at Camden, N.J. October 1975.

R.J. Yanosey

R.J. Yanosey

Robert Malinoski

M.S. Zak Collection

Most would identify a 2100 series GP30 as a former NYC unit, but such is not the case with 2198 and 2199. The former PRR 2250 and '51 were renumbered into these numbers when the first GP35's started to arrive on the Pennsy. (Above) 2198 leads a GP40-C425-U33B lashup west up the "River Line" with 126 cars of NS1 on April 5, 1972 at Teaneck, N.J.

Former PRR 2205 was lucky enough to wear the elusive "red P," and in this photo (left) rounds a curve in Cove, Pa. on March 1, 1970 with westbound empty hoppers.

Based out of Morrisville, Pa. PC 2208 (below) and two look alikes on a Bel-Del freight await recrewing in the yard at Trenton, N.J. July 10, 1971.

M.S. Zak, RJY Collection

After PC assumed ownership of the GP30's, they could be found in both symbol and secondary service. The 10 ex NYC units, lacking dynamic brakes were assigned to Collinwood and its flat terrain. The ex PRR units were scattered in small groups to eastern bases such as Morrisville, Enola, and Conway where they could be found any day working a Flexi-Van train, eastbound at "View" tower, Duncannon, Pa. 7/11/69 (center) or heading up NJ Division locals as seen in these views at Trenton, N.J. 3/31/75 and 6/20/71 (top and bottom, respectively).

M.S. Zak Collection

M.S. Zak Collection

M.S. Zak Collection

33

Herbert H. Harwood

(Above) The "Four Deuces" and a GP9B have a long eastbound cut of RF&P boxcars in hand on the ascending grade at B&P Junction, Baltimore, Md. in March 1973. It was about this time that the GP30 fleet now 10 years old was starting to emerge from major overhauls in this "black dip" scheme, lacking the spelled out "Penn Central" on the long hood.

(Below) Six months after merger date just about any possible combination of PC-PRR-NYC units could be found on the mainline. This shot is a prime example as PC GP30 2229 leads ex PRR FP7 4344 and ex NYC F7 1682 westward out of the "new," 1904 bore at Gallitzin, Pa, August 1968.

William J. Brennan

34

R.J. Yanosey

(Above) Just west (north geographically) of Harrisburg in Marysville, Pa. stood "Banks" tower for over half a century. Aptly named for its location on the west bank of the Susquehanna River, "Banks" was utilized to merge traffic from the ex PRR mainline to and from the busy Enola Yard. Here, only one month after the merger, GP30 2233 already wears PC black, as she guides two oversize flatcars bearing three Army tanks past the tower. By the mid 1980's the locomotive, the tower and the caboose would depart this earth forever. We don't know about the tanks.

(Below) Another example of the interesting power that could be found out there just after the merger looms out of the haze at Perdix, Pa. on July 15, 1968. The eastbound mixed freight is lead by ex PRR 2235 with "red P" and a GP30 mate still in NYC livery. Although that flared dynamic brake blister gave the GP30 its muscular good looks, it remained the same whether or not the unit actually had dynamics underneath. As you would expect PRR purchased GP30's with dynamic brakes in deference to its mountainous terrain, while "water level" NYC did not.

M.S. Zak Collection

R. J. Yanosey

R.J. Yanosey

There was a time when the steel traffic of the Pittsburgh area was so strong, so intense, that the Pennsylvania Railroad felt it necessary to assemble a bypass around the city for through traffic. Much like today's interstates that form rings around major cities, the Conemaugh Line left the ex PRR Main at Johnstown, Pa. and reentered at Federal Street on the northwest side of Pittsburgh. (Above) PC 2236 uses this route as she rounds a curve by the Wean - United Engineering & Foundry building in Vandergrift, Pa., April 1974. Unfortunately, the weeds infesting this mainline were all too common on the railroad at this time. It was taking special "loans" from Congress to enable PC to continue enough track maintenance to keep the road open.

(Left center) 2242 exhibits the handsome nose of the GP30 at Phillipsburg, N.J. November 1974, while (below) 2246 sports the best of the PC's paint schemes at Detroit, December 11, 1968.

J.W. Swanberg

GP35
2250 - 2399

Late in 1963, EMD once again upgraded its road freight units by increasing the horsepower to 2500 and making several other internal improvements which resulted in the new GP35. Gone was the rakish look of the GP30 and in its place there was the beginning of the "spartan" cab phase that was to dominate the external appearance of EMD roadswitchers for at least the next quarter century. Equipped with the 567D3A engine, the GP35 was manufactured from 11/63 until 1/66. During that time PRR purchased 119 GP35's and NYC 31.

RJY Collection

R. J. Yanosey

M.S. Zak Collection

(Top) Externally the GP35 can be distinguished from its look-alike younger relation the GP40, by its shorter length and small radiator fan between two large fans on the rear of the long hood (on GP40's all three are large). Ex PRR 2263 displays this at Conway, Pa. September 21, 1968.

(Center) In March 1968, freshly painted 2277 carries the results of an encounter with a snow bank on her pilot through Renovo, Pa. on the ex PRR Harrisburg to Buffalo Line. Compare the paint on 2277 with the GP9B in PRR paint trailing, and you can see why many debated the "blackness" of "Brunswick green."

(Left) In October 1973, GP35 2278 attended by GP40 3008 hurry empty grain hoppers back to the midwest through Bradenville, Pa. along the ex PRR mainline. PRR had operated through here for over 50 years with 4 tracks; PC would reduce it to 3; Conrail to 2.

37

(Right) 5800 horsepower from GP35 2282 and U33B 2935 propel a mixed freight west through Duncannon, Pa. on June 28, 1969.

M.S. Zak Collection

Herbert H. Harwood

William J. Brennan

(Center) In August 1968, GP35 2309 still in PRR paint, a GE, and an ex NYC GP30 creep out of the portals at Tunnel Hill, Pa. The entire train is at the crest of the Alleghenies, 2200' above sea level and prepared to brake the 11 miles down to 1200' high, Altoona. If the train should exceed maximum speed of 12 mph here the following warning devices will function:

1) Cab signal will indicate approach
2) Eastward home signal at Benny will flash
3) Wayside horn at a point 300' east of MP 247 will sound

and there will be a major "problem" if the engineer doesn't comply!

(Left) September 1973, an eastbound manifest thunders by the station at Dennison, Ohio on the ex PRR Panhandle (Pittsburgh to St. Louis) Line. GP35 2321 does the honors.

The GP35's were quickly identifiable as to previous owner on PC. Although the dividing line in the 148 units came between 2368 (ex PRR) and 2369 (ex NYC), it was easier to simply look for the dynamic brake blister on the long hood of these units. Ex PRR units had them, and with one exception, NYC units did not. This anomaly was the last unit, 2399, which NYC purchased from EMD which had displayed it at the 1964-65 World's Fair in New York.

In the type of picture (right) that must have been imagined by the men who created Penn Central, the Blomberg trucks of GP35 2327 and the high adhesion trucks of Century 430 2058 bite the rails while rounding the park at Horseshoe Curve. This was only five months into the merger, July 1968, and the Century was still in system road service.

(Below) In April 1977, exactly one year after Penn Central exited the railroad game, ex-PC GP35 2338 savors the cool night air at the former Erie Lackawanna engine terminal at Bison Yard, Buffalo along with high hooded N&W U boats

R J. Yanosey

WilliamJ. Brennan

R. J. Yanosey

R. J. Yanosey

(Above) Ex PRR 2349 along with two look alike GP40's and a GP38 storm across the majestic, stone arch, Granville Bridge over the Juniata River west of Lewistown, Pa. in 8/76. Constructed in 1906 when the PRR was four tracking its mainline, the eight stone arches remained untouched until PC found it necessary to reinforce several Juniata bridges with steelwork after the damage caused by tropical storm "Agnes."

(Left) 2376 poses 3/4 illustrating the absence of dynamic brakes on ex NYC GP35's, at Secaucus, N.J. one month after Conrail startup. This ex EL facility was infested with ex PC and EL GP35's during this period as Conrail set up a Secaucus - Buffalo GP35 pool (while taking the ex EL SD45's to the mountains!).

(Below) In March 1970 GP35 2371, GP38 7775, and Century 425 2419 roll through Canton, Ohio. Canton is the final resting place of native son William McKinley and plays host to the Pro Football Hall of Fame. More important to Penn Central, however, its location on the old Pittsburgh Fort Wayne & Chicago (PRR) provided a steady source of traffic from the many specialty steel producers in the area.

Herbert H. Harwood Collection

DL640
2400-2414

The DL640 or RS27 was a rare diesel of which only 27 were manufactured by Alco from 12-59 to 10-62. Of that 27, PRR purchased more than half (15) of these 2400 hp roadswitchers. As you might expect, the DL640 was not a particularly successful locomotive. Although often put into storage during traffic slumps, the PC DL640 fleet did manage to survive until Conrail ownership.

(Top) PC 2401 mingles with other Alcos at Mingo Jct. in October 1976 with not much of a future in store for it.

(Center) In happier days (November 28, 1970) a more simply adorned 2401 leads a GP38, GP30 combo eastbound at Duncannon, Pa.

(Bottom) 2405 is all dressed up in full PC paint with "red P" at Conway, Pa. on June 22, 1969. It seems PC could never figure out where to put the herald on the long hood on DL640's, above the radiators or alongside.

R. J. Yanosey

M. S. Zak Collection

M. S. Zak Collection

41

The scene at left was taken one month into Conrail at the ex EL facility in Secaucus, N.J. (Croxton Yard). TV98 has arrived and the brakeman gets down to bend some iron for the train to properly yard itself. As the younger 6338 looks on, the 2407 appears in charge of not only an important piggyback train but the competition as well under her multiple unit control. The "delighted" ex EL mechanical people had a quick solution for such strange visitors: dispatch them west on the first thing leaving town!

(Below) UBC is a unit coal train bound for the Bethlehem Steel Company at Sparrowbush, Md. On Sunday, October 1, 1972 at "View" the 2407 is once again in charge as she and sister 2412 make easy work of 54 cars of coal at "View" tower. Several years later a similar coal train would derail here destroying the tower building and interlocking; "View" was then rebuilt as a control point.

R. J. Yanosey

Robert Malinoski

D. Hamley, RJY Collection

C424
2415

In April of 1963, Alco introduced its Century 424, a refinement of the DL640 (although both utilized the same 251B engine). In fact, PRR 2415, later PC 2415 (right) was built utilizing the electrical equipment from Alco's scrapped DL640 demonstrator 640-I. This was the one and only unit in this PC class.

42

R. J. Yanosey

R. J. Yanosey

C425
2416 - 2459

Alco tried again in 1964 to come up with a saleable product for the then current boom in replacement locomotives. The Century 425 matched the GE U25B and the GM GP35 in horsepower, but for a number of other reasons would never match their sales. Bitter past experiences with Alco, and standardization on GM and GE products proved more than the C425 could overcome. Of the 91 units produced by Alco from 1964-66, PRR purchased about a third of the production (31) like 2422 (top) at Hollidaysburg, Pa., May 1975.

New Haven's initial order for second generation power (1964) was split between GE (10-U25B's) and Alco (10-C425's). One year later, after comparing both in actual service and seeking more power, NH chose to place its entire order for 16 2500 hp units with GE. Even the most faithful have their limits. C425 2456 (left) was a former NH unit shown at Cedar Hill, October, 1973.

(Below) The home signal at "Banks" has cleared so C425 2417 and an F7B sand the rail to get underway again on March 20, 1971. While the sign cites the Allegheny Division as safest in '68 and '69, that right of way littered with rail, fishplates and spike barrels won't help in '71. Hopefully, the installation of that continuous welded rail was not too long delayed.

M. S. Zak Collection

43

Robert Malinoski

R.J. Yanosey

(Top) Alco power is on the point of a solid 94 car coal train. C425 2427, DL640 2414 and GP35 2370 are passing through Mifflin, Pa. at 5:27 P.M. on Saturday, September 12, 1970. About a half hour behind this train was Berkshire NKP 759 on a fantrip between Harrisburg and Gallitzin, Pa.

(Left) 2436 peers forward at the engine terminal at Cresson, Pa. July 1973.

(Below) After Conrail came into being, the Centuries of all the component roads were gathered together for one last reunion in the Mingo-Cleveland ore pool. Here ex NH C425 2457 and EL C424 2405 are boarded for yet another day's work at Cleveland (EL) October 1976. A lot of things have changed since the last time these two saw Maybrook.

R.J. Yanosey

44

Cresson, Pa. is always an interesting place to check out. Located at MP 251 (Distance from Philadelphia), the small Cresson engine terminal sits atop the Alleghenies next to Gallitzin. The terminal handles not only pushers for the hill but power for two busy coal lines: the Cresson and South Fork Secondaries. In addition, several coal trains a day came from the Bethlehem Steel Mines at nearby Ebensburg via the Cambria & Indiana RR and onto the Cresson Secondary.

On this date in May 1975, two Century 425's have stopped their train across from the engine terminal on account of a mechanical problem with the second unit (left). Problem solved, the train moves on (below), rounding the big curve underneath Route 53 about a mile east.

ALCO

Both, R. J. Yanosey

R. J. Yanosey

For years General Electric had been satisfied with its role as chief supplier of electrical equipment to several non EMD diesel builders. Sales of miniature diesels for shortlines and industries, and the limited manufacturing of electric locomotives seemed like a "safe" niche for giant General Electric (if you were one of those other diesel builders). In the mid fifties, however, ALCO and GM had to raise a corporate eyebrow as GE began building some powerful Turbines for Union Pacific and even worse, rolled out a four diesle cab set apparently

R.J. Yanosey

R.J. Yanosey

designed for domestic mainlines. In early 1959, GE decided to make its play by introducing the unheard of at the time 2500 hp, U25B. The unit was very popular with Penn Central's predecessors who purchased a full one fourth of the entire production of 478. All three proceeded to adopt horsepower/numbering with these 2500 hp units and placed them in the 2500 series. The subsequent merger required an overhaul of that.

(Top) NYC purchased 70 of the GE's, like 2523 at Secaucus, N.J., May 1976, clearly illustrating the flat shorthood of early production models; a classic U25B, built in mid 1964.

PRR's U25B's (59) came in five orders between 1962 and late 1965. Initially numbered in the 2500's the last batch came in the planned PC numbering scheme, like 2653 (center) at Selkirk, N.Y. October, 1973. Note the sloping low nose and split windshield of this later U25B carbody built in December '65.

New Haven contributed 26 U25B's to the PC pool. Two, 2664 and 2661 (right) wear slightly different paint schemes at Selkirk, 10/73. These are also "classic" U25B's with flat noses and large single piece windshields, part of a NH October '64 order for 10 (PC 2660-2669). NH's 1965 order for 16 U25B's (PC 2670-2685) were the later sloped nose, split windshield type.

The U25B is a 60' 2" long diesel weighing about 130 tons, developing a tractive effort of 81,000 pounds. The power is provided by a 2500 hp turbocharged V-16 manufactured by the Cooper-Bessemer Company of Mount Vernon, Ohio. Above, early 1964 production example PC (NYC) 2507 shares the engine terminal at Weehawken, N.J., May 1968, with several different GM, GE and Alco models.

(Right), The U25B from NYC won the right to bear the 2500 number that all three roads once shared. In November 1973, now PC, U25B 2500 leads a coal drag off Rockville Bridge and into Enola Yard.

(Below) Two early competitors, U25B 2625 and GP30 2204, both ex Pennsy, scurry along with a westbound at Cove, Pa., July 13, 1969.

The 67 auto rack cars of ML-12 stretch all the way back under Fort Montgomery tunnel and the Bear Mountain Bridge in this photo. Powered by ex PRR U25B 2646 and ex NYC U30B 2838, the train is at Iona Island, N.Y. on March 10, 1969 on the former NYC West Shore. About 35 more miles south, ML-12 will complete its long journey at Little Ferry, N.J. where the 804 autos will be off loaded for the showrooms of the New York City area. Before the coming of Toyota, Hyundai, Nissan, etc., Detroit could originate many more trains like ML-12.

Robert Malinoski

D.T. Walker

2656 leads fellow GE's west on the Northeast Corridor at Metuchen, N.J. on September 20, 1975. The heritage of the second unit is apparent as the white frame striping of NYC shows thru the peeling PC black.

Robert Malinoski

Three months after New Haven was absorbed into PC (3/16/69 Poughquag, N.Y.) unrenumbered NH 2502 together with PC U33B 2892 and GP40 3206 work Advance OB-2 thru the snow covered landscape. The three units struggle with 87 cars and caboose C-584 up Poughquag hill and are slowly grinding to a halt. Unfortunately, the train stalled and the crew was seen later unabashedly having to use coffee containers to spread sand on the rails.

Robert Malinoski

E.D. Galvin, Herbert H. Harwood Collection

Ray Hubert, Herbert H. Harwood Collection

(Top) After the January 1, 1969 absorption of NH into the PC system, NH power underwent a slow metamorphosis into PC black paint. The New Haven has been merged only about 10 weeks previous to this photo of hot Maybrook to Boston train OB-2. Two pure NH units, U25B 2524 and C425 2551 plus PC U33B 2892 are lugging 84 cars and caboose C-579 up Poughquag hill at 3:45 p.m. on March 9, 1969.

(Center) Several months later, just about any paint scheme could be found on former NH units. As example, in July 1969 the BO-1 passing thru Readville, Ma., has three NH U25B's on the point; 2673 in NH paint with PC number, 2661 ex NH now fully painted PC, and a lead U25B in pure New Haven.

(Bottom) By 1971, new PC President Bill Moore had ordered that all power of predecessor roads have their former names obliterated and PC decals applied in order to achieve unity and common goals. At New Haven, Ct., January 1971, witness the former NH 2525 with that identification removed and PC 2685 applied. Apparently, six months after the bankruptcy, it was not the time to bring up the issue of aesthetics on PC.

R.J. Yanosey

In step with the consensus of American railroads in the early 1970's, the PC moved away from the purchase of high horsepower B-B's and instead turned to intermediate non-turbocharged road-switchers. At the time, General Electric was producing the 2300 hp U23B in response to EMD's popular GP38-2 and PC signed up for a total of 77 of this model in 1972 and '73. The U23B utilized the same carbody as the U30 line but instead was powered by only a thrifty 12 cylinder engine.

(Left) 2746 at Secaucus, N.J., May 1976 was included in PC's 1972 order.

(Below) 2771, a 1973 GE graduate, leads two mates and a grain extra east into Enola Yard, in April 1976. In the background the rocky, mile wide Susquehanna River valley awaits the coming of spring budding, and Conrail.

Herbert H. Harwood

Penn Central operated only 5 U28B's. Two were directly from the former New York Central while the other three 2800 hp, late U25B look alikes, were leased from subsidiary Pittsburgh & Lake Erie. Over the years, many PC U30B's and U33B's have been mistakenly identified as U28B's due to their 2800 series numbers.

(Left, top) P&LE U28B 2809 received a full Penn Central paint job while on lease to PC. It is shown at Newberry Jct., Pa., July 2, 1971.

M.S. Zak Collection

(Left, center) 2810 carries both a PC herald on the nose and P&LE sublettering under the window number while at Enola, August 29, 1971. Both units and 2811 (not shown) were later returned to P&LE.

M.S. Zak Collection

U30B
2830-2889

Late in 1966, General Electric, no doubt feeling obliged to match the horsepower ratings of EMD's recently introduced GP40, upped the horsepower on its U28B and created the 3000 hp U30B. NYC was the only one of the three predecessors of PC that purchased this model.

(Right) The Central legacy of 2881 can be easily discerned from the painted over herald under the window of this U30B at Youngstown, Ohio, June 28, 1969.

M.S. Zak Collection

(Above) Coming off the old West Shore and onto the B&A and Selkirk Yard limits, U30B 2846 is working with two of its GP40 competitors in this November 21, 1971 photo.

(Left) U30B 2855 sports a "paint scheme" that is known to have appeared on several units. The herald on the nose of 2855 appears to have been intended for use on a long hood and is about 4 times as large as the herald on 2846 above, top photo. Unfortunately, the black paint job was all too typical of PC repaints in those days. The center photo shows 2855 at Buttonwood, Pa., 6/20/71, in a weathered but intact black. In the bottom photo, taken three years later July 19, 1974 at Harmon, N.Y., 2855 eastbound on VN-4, still sports her oversize PC herald, but the former NYC oval under the window and white frame striping are starting to show through. Peeling paint, hood doors flapping around, and lack of color often led many fans off PC properties for more colorful, tidier railroads.

PC 2849 brings Amtrak train #72 the "Washington Irving" safely into the terminal at Harmon, N.Y. during a bad snowstorm three days before Christmas 1975. FL9's 5014 and 5013 had failed at Hudson, N.Y. and required the assistance of the 3000 hp GE. The GE's tended to be found on the ex NYC mains radiating out of Selkirk, N.Y. where most U boats were based for maintenance.

J.W. Swanberg

Robert Malinoski

M.S. Zak Collection

NYC, and subsequently PC, scheduled NY-4 out of Chicago every evening with many loads of meats and other perishables. It was due in New York City the second morning. This trip it is running late with ex NYC U30B 2856 and a newer U33B 2890 leading 105 cars including 44 loaded reefers. The train is shown (above) exiting Breakneck Tunnel, Cold Spring, N.Y. on the former NYC Hudson Division at 12:49 p.m. March 10, 1969.

(Left) 2857 at Rutherford, Pa., 3/9/77, illustrates a U30B in full PC paint. The diesel has little time left under Conrail ownership.

53

Six 4 axle GE's (2858-2864-2901-2913-2520-2954) lead NG-3 up the Hudson Valley at Crugers, N.Y. July 5, 1976 (left). Careful identification is in order; while quick visual sighting of the number 2858 would place it squarely in the middle of the U30B block (2830-2889), it turns out 2858 is actually one of the two ex NYC U33B's, making this a powerful U33B-U30B-U33B-U33B-U25B-U33B combo.

(Below, center) LS-1 has always been the New York Central's premier boxcar merchandise train from New York City to Chicago. U30B 2861, GP40 3146 and U30B 2874 have 133 cars well in tow through the flatlands west of Conneaut, Ohio. The train consists of 55 box cars of forwarder merchandise from Universal and Western Carloading Companies, plus 20 empty reefers and 55 mixed freight followed by caboose 21531. The time and date: 4:37 p.m. Wednesday, October 9, 1968.

(Bottom) The short consist of TV42 confirms the forthcoming abandonment of the unsuccessful experiment of a North Bergen, N.J. - Buffalo piggyback service. U30B 2875 singly handles 2 cars, caboose 24511, 2 more pigs and working caboose 24539 on the River Line thru Teaneck, N.J. at 8:48 a.m. on Wednesday, April 5, 1972.

J.W. Swanberg

Robert Malinoski

Robert Malinoski

U33B
2890-2970

In 1967 GE once again improved on its B-B roadswitcher by raising the horsepower 10% to 3300. Quickly identifiable by the large radiator "wings" on the rear of the long hood, the U33B's were the first GE B-B's purchased new by Penn Central. PC 2942 (right) models at Kearny, N.J., November 1974.

(Center, below) 2890, the first number in the PC bought U33B series, leads mixed eastbound tonnage through Morning Sun (East Vandergrift), Pa in August 1974. The boro got the Morning Sun moniker late in the nineteenth century when an early resident who occupied property adjoining the beautiful Kiskiminetas River was so awe struck by the beauty of the morning sun's rays as they glinted off the river through his vineyard, that he decided to give that name to the little town.

(Bottom) U33B 2893 heads a seven unit lashup of GE and GM low nosed products with a westbound freight around the humpyard at Selkirk, N.Y. October, 1973. Unfortunately, the seven unit lashup was not atypical of the way PC powered some freights, as extra units were often hung on, not for tonnage or speed reasons, but to ensure at least 4 units would always "stay on line" to get the train over the road. Such "wasteful" dispatching of power on the single tracked all important, River Line, was considered prudent on a railroad which conducted "maintenance by crisis".

R.J. Yanosey

R.J. Yanosey

R.J. Yanosey

U33B 2895 and a 2870 series U30B curve eastward with empty hoppers past the U.S. Steel mill in Vandergrift, Pa., August 1974. Vandergrift was named after Jacob J. Vandergrift, one of the early pioneer refiners in western Pennsylvania's 19th Century oil boom. The radiator "wing" difference between a U33B and a U30B is readily apparent in this photo.

R.J. Yanosey

RJY Collection

Herbert H. Harwood

In the center photo above, U33B 2897 and friends exit the Indiana Harbor Belt's Argo Yard with tonnage on January 31, 1970. Argo is the IHB yard which services the EMD plant that created the other units in this train. Also served is Pielet Brothers where many of the diesels to be scrapped in America meet their fate, making Argo a virtual Mecca for diesel fans.

At right, U33B 2917 and a GP40 power an eastbound TV train on the former NYC main thru North East, Pa., July 1971. The 2917 eventually became B&M power after being sold to the Guilford road in March 1986 . While North East is located in the northwest corner of Pennsylvania, it is more precisely in the northeast portion of the triangle which juts up from Pa. to separate N.Y. from Ohio. The NYC main hugged Lake Erie here enroute from Buffalo to Cleveland.

Robert Malinoski

Mail #10 (top) is drifting down the mountain past Horseshoe Curve and now is astride Scotch Run curve (MP 241) at 9:21 a.m. on Tuesday, October 19, 1971. The train consists of U33B 2920, GP40's 3063 and 3030, a deadhead coach, 23 Flexi Vans, deadhead sleeper, UP "Pacific Patrol", and passenger service cabin 4710. Actually the term "cabin" became outlawed on Penn Central, to end yet another argument . . . this time whether to call that car a "caboose" (NYC term) or "cabin" (PRR). Caboose won.

(Center) 2948 brings a southbound freight down the former PRR Bel-Del Line at Scudder's Falls, N.J., January 2, 1970. The snow on the ground bears mute testimony to the monkey wrench all PC operations were in that month. 2948 and the former NH units are strangers to this line and are attempting to complete a detour occasioned by the bad weather in the northeast. To the right of the Bel-Del, lies the Delaware and Raritan Canal. Now a pleasure for canoeists, the canal was built in the 1820's to haul Pennsylvania coal east. During the Civil War over 100 coal barges a day traversed it, pulled by sure-footed mules on the towpaths. 75 feet wide and 8 feet deep, the canal was hand shoveled out by Irish immigrants, many of whom died in a cholera epidemic and were buried alongside.

(Bottom) In 1971, however, Pennsylvania coal had an easier, if less picturesque way to get to market. Here the 8700 "mule-power" of this GE-EMD-Alco combination moves a mile of black gold eastward at Cove, Pa., March 20, 1971.

M.S.Zak Collection

M.S.Zak Collection

3000 Series: GP40's and B units

GP40
3000-3274

In 1966 EMD commenced a wholesale revision of its locomotive line. Abandoning the 567 engine which was the basis for its its success, EMD introduced its new 645 engine with the GP40. Equipped with an a.c.-rectifier transmission, the new GP40 immediately won its initial order from New York Central and was subsequently reordered by that road for a total of 105 units.

M.S.Zak Collection

Robert Malinoski

Herbert H. Harwood

(Top) PC 3027 came in the first production batch of GP40's ordered by NYC very late in 1965. Shown at Camden, N.J., January 31, 1970.

(Center) NYC people called their Flexi Van trains "Super Vans." This particular SV-6 was flying low thru Conneaut, Ohio on October 9, 1968 behind GP40 3011 and three companions. After the eight Flexi Vans on the head end came 47 more mixed pigs and vans followed by caboose 21030.

(Left) GP40 3042 leads a real mixed bag . . . NYC GP40-PC GP40-PC U33B-PC U25B-PRR GP35-NYC F7A . . . west at Northumberland, Pa. in June of 1969. Note that the second unit GP40 3011, seen in the center photo above, is now in full Penn Central dress.

R.J.Yanosey

Elmer Treloar, Herbert H. Harwood Collection

(Top) GP40 3043 and 2 U boats clip past the majestic ex NYC station at Gary, Indiana in May 1968. Their long run will end in just a few miles in Chicago, as Gary sits astride the Illinois - Indiana border. Once one of the most uninhabited and desolate areas on Lake Michigan, Gary was the brainchild of Judge Elbert Gary, chairman of U.S. Steel in 1906, when the city was founded. Judge Gary purchased 6000 acres in 1905 and then proceeded to build the world's second largest steel mill along with an accompanying city for the workers.

(Center) Railroads often use standard plans for building structures throughout their systems. At North East, Pa. in July 1971, 3058 "opens it up" passing the "standard plan" old Lake Shore & Michigan Southern RR station in town.

(Left) Further west on the old LS&MS a similar standard station at Sandusky, Ohio is passed by another GP40; this time the 3072 westbound, October 1973.

59

With the exception of the first five units (3100-3104), all the GP40's in the 3100 and 3200 series were purchased by Penn Central in 1968-1970. PC 3137 (right, top) is an example posed at the D&H's Hudson, Pa. yard in fall 1973.

R.J. Yanosey

(Center) GP40 3115 and friend tote a hopper train east on the Conemaugh Line; PRR's version of a "water level" route, which hugs the banks of the Conemaugh, Kiskiminetas, and Allegheny Rivers from Johnstown to Pittsburgh, Pa. In this photo taken in May 1975, to the left of the train lies the boro of East Vandergrift, to the right the banks of the Kiskiminetas. Riverbanks throughout this area are overgrown with "cow weed," a tenacious vine liberated by a floating PRR boxcar carrying the imported feed during the 1936 "Johnstown flood."

(Below) The "op" hands up the flimsies to the engineer aboard GP40 3124 as the train keeps rolling west. This typical ex NYC "Big Four" tower is "Grafton" in the town of that name in Ohio, July 1970. The formal name of this ex NYC subsidiary, absorbed long ago, is Cleveland, Cincinnati, Chicago & St. Louis Railroad; hence the "Big Four" nickname.

R.J. Yanosey

Herbert H. Harwood

Elmer Treloar, Herbert H. Harwood Collection

Elmer Treloar, Herbert H. Harwood Collection

GP40 3126 has help from elder sister GP35 2263 to bring a mixed assortment of freight south near Erie, Michigan in February 1973. The future held a lot more snow for 3126. In late 1983, just as its 15 year trust expired, the lessor sold the GP40 to the D&RGW. It would have been ironic had one of the GP40's sold been built on the trade in credit of a 1970 D&RGW-PC F7.

(Right) The signal and "smashboard" are very clear on Rule 292 : STOP! Eastbound GP40 3129 cools her wheels at the Maumee River Bridge in Toledo, August 1972. Toledo was an extremely important point to Penn Central, not only for the many industries and interchanges in the area, but for the convergence of the east-west mains with the lines to the all important, automobile producing, Detroit area. Respecting this meshing of traffic, Toledo became the first major terminal area truly merged under PC with yard consolidations and new labor agreements

(OPPOSITE PAGE - TOP) GP40 3129, the same one seen on the previous page stopped at the Maumee River bridge, is much more active in this photo at Turtle Creek, Pa in October 1975. Obviously, either the Amtrak SDP40F or E8 had had a failure and were in need of assistance to bring train #30, "The National Limited" across the rugged terrain of western Pennsylvania ahead. The 3129 probably stayed on all the way to Harrisburg where a trusty GG-I would be waiting (R.J. Yanosey)

(Opposite Page-center) The Hudson River forms one of the finest backgrounds in the U.S.for train action photos. PC train EV-2 (Enola to Selkirk) has come around Jones Point and will shortly be at Iona Island and then Bear Mountain. Six units 3168, 2221, 2297, 2274, 2558 and 3269 have the 138 cars plus ex PRR caboose 23256 well in hand at 12:35 p.m. on Sunday, April 11, 1971. You can always tell a Bob Malinoski shot. They are not only excellent, well posed scenes taken by a master photographer, but Bob highlights his work with a ream of data on the train makeup: symbol, consist, location, date and even the time. Young photographers take heed !

(Opposite Page-bottom) Another Malinoski portrait is created as Mail #10 passes "Port" tower just west of Newport, Pa. at 11:12 a.m. on Sunday, September 13, 1970. Power is 3 GP40's with lead unit 3182 featuring a rare "orange C" in the PC logo. (Only GP40's 3170 - 3186 wore this scheme right out of La Grange for several years. One RS3 5585, an ex NH unit, had a partial "orange C" rendition. The rest of the train consists of the 3207, 3137 and 25 Flexi Vans of mail and 2 cabins (cabooses!).

(THIS PAGE-TOP), the PC bought GP40's extended out of the 3100 series and well into the 3200's (to 3274), such as 3205 (top, right) at Mingo Jct., October 1976.

(Center, right) Here the same 3205, over 7 years earlier, heads south with 70 cars of coal for the nearby Tompkins Cove, N.Y. power plant. In the background of this Valentine's Day, 1969 photo, some of the WWII Liberty ships, which had been anchored there for two decades, are clearly visible. They had experimented using them for storage of grain purchased by the U.S. Goverment under various farm subsidy plans, but by this time their only future lies in scrap yards down the Hudson.

(Right, bottom) PC-B&M pool train NY-10 has an interesting matchup in April 1975 at Rotterdam Jct., N.Y. as PC GP40 3212 leads 2 B&M F7B units east. Ironically, B&M would purchase some ex PC GP40's in 1985, but not the 3212.

R.J. Yanosey

Robert Malinoski

J. Armstrong, Herbert H. Harwood Collection

(Top) Penn Central 3213 and companion bring a westbound past the ex Erie RR station at Galion, Ohio in April 1973. Penn Central's "Big Four" and Erie Lackawanna had a paired track arrangement between Galion and Marion, Ohio during this time.

Elmer Treloar, Herbert H. Harwood Collection

(Center) GP40 3216 has a roll on a westbound on the former NYC's Canada Southern RR thru Essex, Ontario in August 1970. From this point in time on, the Canada Southern would continually deteriorate as PC was unable to give it half the track maintenance it deserved.

(Below) The 3229 and a GE bring a solid train of culvert pipe west across venerable Rockville Bridge on May 31, 1969.

Elmer Treloar, Herbert H. Harwood Collection

M.S. Zak Collection

M.S. Zak Collection

FB

3323-3397

About 20 ex NYC Alco B units arrived at Penn Central's doorstep February 1968. PC foresaw that the units would not be long for this world, so they did not repaint the units which retained their NYC paint like FB2 3366 (above). 3366, incidentally, did not make Penn Central by a few months - photographed at Collinwood March 11, 1967. Trade ins for new U33B's caused the ex NYC FB's numbers to diminish to about a half dozen by early 1969.

The ex NH units saw longer life, however, thanks to an in kind rebuilding by Alco 10 years earlier and a low mileage run in the Boston area. Repainted FB2 3393 (below), the ex NH 465, idles at Lamberton Street, New Haven, Ct., August 16, 1970.

J.W. Swanberg

F7B
3429-3563

Back in the late 40's and early 50's the railroads were sold on the building block principle of a "nose" (A unit) on the front and rear of a diesel, and as many blocks (B units) as necessary, in between. Many roads went back to EMD just for more B units when they saw they needed more power, but most roads had purchased their B units as part of a 4500 or 6000 hp "locomotive." Later, as the roads became more adept diesel buyers and the switch to hood units was on, railroads found they could use the B units in any place in a lashup, except of course, in the lead.

D. Hamley, R. J. Y. Collection

M.S. Zak Collection

D. Hamley, R. J. Y. Collection

The 3439 (top) at Conway, Pa. and the 3440 (center) at Enola 10/11/69 are examples of ex NYC F7B units in Penn Central paint.

(Left) The 3478 spent most of the previous 15 years adorned in golden yellow and silver paint, climbing the steep slopes of the Rocky Mountains. Now the ex D&RGW F7B wears a more somber coat of PC black and works the flat country out of Collinwood, Ohio.

R.J. Yanosey

GP9B
3800-3839

Pennsy was able to kill off steam by purchasing hundreds of 1750 hp EMD GP9's during the late fifties. Since sets of four or five GP9's provided the premier power on the PRR in those days, it seemed logical to the road to ease the capital cost of this betterment by eliminating cabs for the center units. PRR even came back to EMD for 10 more GP9B's in late 1959 when it needed more power and steam had already been dead for two years. A decade later, however, GP9's were no longer top of the line road power and under PC ownership the inflexible GP9B units found themselves demoted to secondary road freights and hump service.

(Above) PC 3826 is shut down awaiting its fate outside the Samuel Rea Shops at Hollidaysburg, Pa. in August 1976. Conrail didn't think too much of the units; and, although Hollidaysburg had locomotive dismantling facilities, more likely 3826 was used for its trade in value at EMD.

(Bottom) In a highly unusual shot, 3839 with headlite burning, leads a westbound at Morrisville, Pa., May 28, 1970. Apparently, the E44 was original power on the train but then had some problem which necessitated dropping the pan and getting the GP9 and GP9B off an eastbound freight and out for a rescue. When the main is blocked on the Northeast Corridor, anything available is grabbed.

M.S. Zak Collection

4000 Series: Passenger Cab Units & Electrics

Lee Hastman, Herbert H. Harwood Collection,

The E7 was the EMD 2000 hp passenger cab unit developed and produced after World War II until 1949. This reliable workhorse quickly convinced purchasers PRR and NYC that EMD passenger units were far ahead of anything to be offered by the other builders; consequently, both roads standardized on the E7 and successor E8 for the bulk of their through train service. By the time of Penn Central, the E7 ranks were diminishing as the systemwide cutback in passenger service allowed the more modern E8's to handle the remaining tasks.

(Top) In June 1970, E7 4006 built in 1945 poses in NYC grey with PC worm at Chicago. 4006 was one of the earliest NYC E7's that were received with the old style number boards.

(2nd from top) 4008 an April 1947 product of EMD (Harrisburg, Pa. 3/20/71) shows where the NYC was painted out and wears the more predominant large number boards.

(3rd from top) 4027 is a good example of what a railroad recently bankrupt is apt to spend on money losing passenger locomotives – not very much! It's July 1970 in Chicago and PC has more pressing problems.

(Bottom) 4029 was one of the lucky NYC E7's to escape such haphazard repaint jobs and received the full treatment. 4029 was manufactured in February 1948, and now it's twenty years and millions of miles later at Conway, Pa., Columbus Day, 1968.

M.S. Zak Collection

Lee Hastman, Herbert H. Harwood Collection

M. S. Zak Collection

One of the best sanctuaries for the ex PRR E7 was the unique New York & Long Branch RR which extended from CNJ and PC railheads in the Amboys to Bayhead, N.J. Along this "Jersey Coastline", both CNJ and PC operated commuter trains bound for the Newark, N.J. or New York City job markets. A long time habitue of this railroad was E7 4233, a spring 1949 graduate of EMD's La Grange production plant.

(Above) Eight months after the Penn Central merger except for the PC number you couldn't tell anything had happened as far as 4233 was concerned. Here the unit waits for "two" while New York newspapers are thrown off the southbound train at the station in Asbury Park, N.J. by a "BMTC" (Baggageman –Ticket Collector).

(Below) On a hot July weekend in 1974, 4233 now in PC's hue is shutdown for the weekend at Bayhead Yard. SOP on weekends was to let the really big trains stay put unless some unusual demand arose.

(Center) It's now four years later (South Amboy, N.J. June 1978), ten years after the Asbury Park shot was taken and almost thirty since 4233 was built. Now owned by the NJ Department of Transportation, 4233's only reward came at Naporano Iron & Metal Company, several months later.

E8
4003-4328

M.S. Zak Collection

RJY Collection,

In the summer of 1949, EMD released an improved passenger unit called the E8. Numerous internal improvements plus an additional 250 hp made the twin V-12 powered diesel a certain winner. Already shown that the passenger cabs offered by Alco-GE, Baldwin and FM were not equal to the E7, NYC and PRR signed up for large orders of E8's. The PC numbering scheme for E units was based around New York Central's which had always been in the 4000's. (PRR's E's were in 5700-5800 series).

(Top) PC 4063 is a May 1953 ex NYC unit seen at Chicago April 28, 1976. Its purpose in Chicago at this date 5 years into Amtrak was for use on the Valparaiso commuter train. When that train was dropped, 4063 came east to the NY&LB.

(Center) E8 4073 out at Toledo, Ohio, June 17, 1972 shows her NYC heritage more than her PC ownership. Unfortunately, PC often chose right after bankruptcy to allow its most visible diesels, the passenger cabs, out in extremely ragged paint. Was this lack of interest and/or money; or a clever political ploy to spotlight the problem?

(Below) NYC had attempted to reduce its substantial passenger operations by initiating "Empire Service" late in the sixties. Empire Service allowed the railroad to lop off much of the service west of Buffalo (and to a degree west of Albany) by substituting several coaches and an E8 for the huge streamliners with Pullmans and diners. This "half a loaf" approach, allowed NYC – and later PC– to produce some genuine savings in a politically difficult area. Here the 4036 has 5 cars in tow southbound through Beacon, N.Y. in June 1968. Note the herald on 4036. Some early PC nose heralds were longer, and consequently harder to discern from a distance than later versions.

William J. Brennan and R.J. Yanosey

(Above) Amtrak would arrive none too soon for the folks who wanted to ride the Boston & Albany. PC 4042 has only one coach in tow at Framingham, Mass. in April 1971, serving as a connection from B&A points to the Empire Service and thru trains at Albany, N.Y. It would be reasonable to say, the GM assembly plant at Framingham was more important to PC than a coach accomodation.

(Right) An Empire Service train headed by ex NYC E8 4044 rests at its terminus at Rensselaer, N.Y. August 2, 1969.

(Bottom) In June 1968, Hollywood came to the Hudson Division and changed the appearance of the ex NYC station at Garrison, N.Y. for the Barbra Streisand movie, "Hello Dolly". It was "made up" to appear as Yonkers, N.Y. looked like years ago as envisioned by some California set designers. They even carried the Penn Central theme to a new end, by utilizing ex PRR 4-4-0 1223 as a New York Central & Hudson River steamer for their scenes. PC 4056 and a couple of coaches on a westbound Empire train, however, restore some reality to all the falsework.

M.S. Zak Collection

Empire Service again. Freshly painted 4068 (left) has one of those flattened (stepped on ?) worms and, hopefully, a few coachloads of southbound passengers at the Movable Bridge at New Hamburg, N.Y. in April 1968. New Hamburg is located about 8 mile south of Poughkeepsie on the Hudson Division.

William J. Brennan

E8 4082 leads a gaggle of 2 NYC E7's and a PRR E8 east with Mail train #4 at Schenectady, N.Y. in April 1968. The Flexi Van service originated by the NYC would eventually lose favor with Penn Central, mostly due to lack of acceptance by other railroads, thus limiting growth through interchange. "Stack Pack" a similiar 1980's concept, perhaps will vindicate the progressive thinking of those NYC planners.

William J. Brennan

John Strombeck, Herbert H. Harwood Collection

Amtrak train 361 makes a station stop at Niles, Michigan in March 1972 with leased PC 4092 doing the honors.

The closest thing NH had to an E unit was its roster of 60 FL9's. At Harmon (top), February 16, 1972, E8 4047 and an FL9 are both dead, but offer a good opportunity to compare the lengths and trucks of the EMD's.

(Center) On the banks of the wide Hudson River, Amtrak train #68 "The Adirondack" passes by the little town of Manitou, N.Y. on July 2, 1975. A very scenic view, indeed, for the passengers in the four coaches headed for the "Big Apple" and ample evidence of why this was dubbed "The Hudson Division."

(Bottom) At New Haven, Ct. on April 7, 1974, Penn Central FL9 5059 and Amtrak E8 279 (still in PC paint) match their bulldog noses while waiting for southbound traffic.

William J. Brennan

In the several years before Amtrak's inception Penn Central was obliged to maintain the most extensive passenger service of any line in the United States. While the aficionado saw a lot of romance in this service, the railroad saw only red ink. Unable to drop passenger service as the demand simply disappeared, the financially ailing company tried to stop the rising tide of deficits by cutting back on outlays wherever possible. This in turn bought forth the wrath of the riding public and, in turn, the state legislatures; a vicious cycle which went on until Amtrak took the yoke.

Casting that aside, however, back to the romantic side of things as Penn Central passenger service is pictured here in the State Capitols of New York (Albany, April 1968 above) and Pennsylvania (Harrisburg, July 1968 below). Fittingly enough, the proper E8 for each state is on its train.

William J. Brennan

R. J. Yanosey

Pennsy was also an enthusiastic buyer of EMD's E8. In PC days, just like the F7, the lifting rings on that bulldog nose were the instant clue to PRR parentage. PC 4285 (left) started life as PRR 5885A back in March 1950. Now, 24 years later, 4285 no longer pulls the Blue Ribbon fleet. Spurned by Amtrak, the unit is assigned to the NY&LB service, but this weekend in November 1974 the unit sits in Kearny, N.J. having spent the last several days traveling to and from Harrisburg, Pa. to receive monthly inspection. Four or more E units on the mail trains, being ferried for M.I., were always something to look out for.

(Center) The acrid smell of brakeshoe dust fills the air as "The Duquesne" slides east into Horseshoe in July 1968. The three cars are more than adequately powered by three E8's including center unit 4249 which has been de-portholed and given a "red P" PC paint job.

(Bottom) In October 1969, "The South Wind" with PC 4252 in the lead, rests at the station in Louisville, Ky. under a threatening sky.

William J. Brennan

Chas. Conniff, Herbert H. Harwood Collection

75

E8 4275 was born in late spring 1952. For the first 16 years of her life under the aegis of PRR and early into successor PC, 4257 has toiled along the passenger routes of the "P" Company, as shown in the photo (right) as she prepares to once again assault the torturous grades of the Alleghenies ahead at Altoona, Pa. in July 1968 with Mail #9.

In the center photo below, three years have passed and Penn Central has more fully integrated its locomotives and operations. The same 4275, now shorn of her portholes, was wearing a coat of PC black, this day in August 1971 and plying ex NH rails thru Canton, Mass. The stone archway carrying 4275 and the west bound mail express is one of the oldest large stone railroad viaducts extant in America. Located on the ex NH Boston - Providence mainline, Canton Viaduct was built in 1835, equalling in age B&O's Thomas Viaduct. It was constructed by the civil engineer of B&A tunnel fame, George Washington Whistler, who later went off to work and die in St. Petersburg, Russia.

William J. Brennan, RJY Collection

Herbert H. Harwood

Herbert H. Harwood

(Right) After the NH was absorbed into the Penn Central system, the ambidexterous FL9's were shifted down to the ex NYC commuter lines out of New York. In return the New Haven Region received a flotilla of excess PRR E8's to haul the passenger trains above New Haven, Ct. In this photo, a tattered 4260 looking as if it had been "prepped" for repainting, instead of service, handles the "New Yorker" at New London, Ct. in July 1969.

(Top) In the middle of a hot afternoon in August 1973, Amtrak train #177 "The Senator" departs South Station, Boston behind Penn Central E8 4261. The heat can be attested to by the "air conditioning" efforts of the engine crew who have left the nose door just slightly ajar in order to scoop in some breeze as they slip down the NEC to New Haven. Many assume the term Northeast Corridor came into being with the Amtrak takeover in 1976. In fact, Penn Central formed "The Northeast Corridor Region" out of the Eastern and Northeastern Regions in 1974-75 in order to better isolate and capture the costs of this expensive territory.

(Left) The fireman on 4264 bringing #178 into the NEC station at Kingston, R.I. gives a friendly wave to the photog on the overhead bridge, June 1974.

(Below) The 2250 hp of a single E8, PC 4284 is sufficient to keep the four cars at track speed thru "View" interlocking at Duncannon, Pa., May 29, 1971. "View" is a good example of the monosyllable names PRR gave to its towers when it replaced the telegrapher's initials earlier in this century. The name usually carried historic or local interest; in this case a magnificent view of the wide Susquehanna River which ran alongside the railroad and tower here.

E8 4290 a 1950 General Motors product, is shown at work in these two photos: at right, 4290 eases into the curve at the west end of Rockville Bridge with four westbound passenger cars on October 11, 1969. The tracks curving to the left side of the photo lead to Altoona and the west. The track to the right brings a train into Enola Yard.

In the center photo below, in May 1968, 4290 ferries two extra units between itself and the Washington, D.C. section of "The Broadway Limited". #548 was separated from the "Broadway" at Harrisburg, Pa. and now has arrived at Baltimore, Md. before heading south for 40 more miles to the nation's capital.

M. S. Zak Collection

Herbert H. Harwood

Herbert H. Harwood

PC 4296, urgently in need of some paint, brings the abbreviated consist of train #53 to a halt at Massillon, Ohio in July 1970. Massillon is located about 8 miles west of Canton on the old PFt.W&C, the ex PRR mainline to Chicago. Everything in this photo has seen better days.

78

(Right) Pennsy experimented with oscillating lights for its passenger diesels by equipping an E8 and a Baldwin shark passenger unit with the feature. Still bearing the extra headlite of that test, PC 4300 has had the oscillating light blanked out, as it prepares for departure from one of Penn Central's three Chicago terminals; this one, the least used, Illinois Central's Central Station.

(Below) The westbound "Duquesne" is approaching Newport, Pa. at 12:06 p.m. on Sunday, September 13, 1970. 4303 and companion make easy work of the five car train on the ex PRR "Middle Division" which hugs the Juniata River almost all the way to Altoona. A right of way that once bore track three and countless trains now only retains the ballast and some scrub weeds as testimony.

RJY Collection

Robert Malinoski

"Red P" 4312 and consist is dwarfed in the massive terminal at Buffalo, N.Y. on September 27, 1969 with train #574 for Harrisburg. The tower building in the background housed not only division headquarters but the Centralized Traffic Control board that governed all mainline operations on the ex NYC trackage in this area.

(Below) #16, "The Dudquesne" once again, is spotted heading east thru Mifflin, Pa. with E8's 4313 and 4282 on this Saturday, September 12, 1970.

J.W. Swanberg

Robert Malinoski

Lee Hastman, Herbert H. Harwood Collection

For Amtrak's inauguration day, May 1, 1971, the NRPC public relations people thought it would be beneficial to paint a passenger locomotive "Amtrak". PC 4316 was chosen to wear this unique, one of a kind, paint scheme although the locomotive was still technically owned by Penn Central. Shown at Chicago (right) one month later, the ex PRR 5716 would soon wear yet another paint scheme and number when it later left the PC roster for Amtrak ownership.

E7B
4100-4126

As Pennsy and Central emerged from the steam era, they learned the hard way in their diesel purchasing. Both managements felt the 4000 hp of two E7A's was not sufficient for some of the 16-20 car streamliners they commonly ran during this period and so filled the gap with E7B purchases. Interestingly, this thinking was not carried thru by either road in later years, as neither road purchased E8B's. (Right) PC 4126 is an ex PRR unit stored serviceable at Harrisburg, March 28, 1970.

M.S. Zak Collection

D. Hamley, RJY Collection

F7B (passenger)
4151-4159

In deference to the rugged Alleghenies and in an attempt to have some dual purpose units for traffic swings between the freight and passenger departments, PRR had purchased 40 FP7 (A units) and 14 passenger equipped F7B's. The B units were simply F7B's with steam lines (there is no such animal as a "FP7B"). The 4156 lasted right into Conrail and is shown in the photo (above, center) at Conway, Pa. in 1976. Earlier, in her Penn Central career the unit looked like this (left) at Enola, Pa. April 7, 1969.

81

R.J. Yanosey

The 4333 (top), was delivered in Tuscan Red instead of the Brunswick Green that most of her siblings wore. It poses at Cresson, Pa., November 1973.

FP7 4337 often appeared lashed up to a high horsepower relative if you can judge from these photos. (Below, middle) The 4337 and NYC GP40 3015 combine for 4500 horses on this hopper train at Northumberland, Pa., in June 1969. In the bottom photo, 4337 grinds upgrade with a PRR SD40 and a hopper train thru Sugar Run Gap, Tunnelhill, Pa., May 4, 1969

The 40 FP7's had spent the earlier parts of their careers fulfilling their billing as dual purpose units. During the Penn Central era these ex PRR diesels were utilized exclusively in freight service, however, and eventually had their steam generators and water tanks removed. Perhaps due to the lighter service of their youth as a group the units survived into Penn Central completely intact.

(OPPOSITE PAGE) The 4353 and mates are covering their sides with silicon dust from the sanding necessary to keep this long string of merchandise traffic in motion. The train is stretched out around Horseshoe Curve in the background in this dramatic August 1968 photo by William J. Brennan. What can't be shown is the raucous cacophony of sound raised by these locomotives as they strain to reach the top of the Allegheny Mountains.

Herbert H. Harwood, RJY Collection

M.S. Zak Collection

R.J. Yanosey

(Above) PC FP7 4345 and a mix of hood units lead a freight south off the Southwest Secondary Track and into the yard at Youngwood, Pa. in August 1974. The Southwest Secondary Track left the former PRR mainline west of Greensburg, PA. at "RG" Interlocking and ran due south to connections with PC's Greensburg, Yukon, and Scottdale Secondary Tracks as well as the B&O in Connellsville.

(Left) FP7 4354, still in PRR livery, leads a "red P" F7 and a NYC U boat east thru Newport, Pa. on February 2, 1969. Common practice on the former PRR when the railroad was elevated was to build the station down at ground level such as Newport's. This allowed for underground passageways to gain access to the other side of the tracks and for autos to drive right up to the station building for passenger pick-up and delivery.

(Below) Shiny FP7 4365 and F7 1740 handle the WM and N&W interchange chores for Penn Central at Hagerstown, Md. in June 1968.

M.S. Zak Collection

Herbert H. Harwood, RJY Collection

E44
4400-4465

The boxy, powerful E44's that Pennsy purchased to replace older electrics in the early 60's continued their dependable service under Penn Central ownership. It seemed that when the diesels were failing one by one due to lack of maintenance, PC could always depend on the high pitched whine of the E44's to bring the freight in. The 4400 hp E44's were unremarked units which seemed to need only sand and juice to keep running forever. Penn Central had other problems more pressing, and did not even wash or paint many of these, instead merely giving them the interim "decal" jobs.

(At right) Dusty but always dependable 4402 leads a freight west over the Passaic & Harsimus Branch and past the engine terminal of the Lehigh Valley in March 1973. Like the "sounds" of the FP7 on page 83, what you can't see in this photo is the horrific smell of the animal fat rendering factories adjacent to the railroad here, making this photo out of the question in July and August.

(Below) PC 4438 illustrated a rare clean and fully painted E44 at Kearny, N.J., January 1977.

R.J. Yanosey

R.J. Yanosey

E44's fore and aft bask in low sunlight on a March afternoon in 1972 at the Kearny, N.J. motor pit.

R.J. Yanosey

M.S. Zak Collection

R.J. Yanosey

Merchandise freights rarely required more than 2 E44's, and this train, (above center) eastbound on track 3 thru the station at Trenton, N.J., is no exception. Trenton was the meeting point for commuter service sponsored by both NJ DOT and SEPTA. The PC MP-54 MU's are on the SEPTA yard side of the railroad, headed to Philadelphia.

(At left) The 4427 and a dirty friend make their entrance onto the Northeast Corridor at "Lane" tower, Newark, N.J. in June 1973. The train was made up in Waverly Yard and is heading west. Waverly was vacated soon after Conrail in favor of the ex LV Oak Island yard in Newark.

86

When the heavy, stiff trucked E44 and E33 electrics left the mainlines of the Penn Central, it was time to keep your fingers crossed. Certainly, Penn Central earned the dubious, derailment championship every year of its existence as lack of track maintenance disseminated the terms "low joint," "wide gauge," "deteriorated ties" and "spread rail" throughout reports all over the system. On October 19, 1975 at Edison, N.J., E44 4436 (left) has derailed on the yard trackage leading to the Ford Motor Company and PC personnel are getting out the time honored, wood blocks in preparation for pulling the engine back and up onto the rail. Standard operating procedure requires that before all this starts, however, an "A" man (Electric Traction Dept) must first arrive and tie the pantograph down with rope. Since the rail provides the return for the current, a badly derailed electric, uncoupled with pantograph up, might use the first human touching it as a ground.

D.T. Walker

Herbert H. Harwood

D.T. Walker

One of the few non-mineral trains to regularly draw three E44's was the eastbound "Juice Train." This train was not only very heavy, but reportedly difficult to handle, being restricted to 65 or less white, insulated, TPIX boxcars from the Tropicana Company in Bradenton, Florida. Restricted by Timetable Special Instructions to 40 mph in several mainline locations and with rear end helpers prohibited, Penn Central gingerly moved "The Juice" from Pot Yard to the Tropicana staging yard at Kearny, N.J. where distribution to the New York market was conducted by truck. After emptying, the cars would return to Florida in 5-10 car groups within regular freights. In the center photo above, the 4439 and two mates bring "Florida Sunshine" thru Baltimore, in May 1972.

(At right) 4409 and 4454 provide an excellent view of the top of an E44, as they wait at "Lane" for a slot to make the same move as the train on the opposite page, bottom. October 16, 1977.

87

A few of the E44's were even adorned with "red P's" during that phase in 1968. 4448 (top) speeds a westbound thru Frankford Jct, Pa. on July 21, 1972, while 4443 (center) brings freight east on a dismal September 26, 1971 at Trenton, N.J.

J.W. Swanberg

M.S. Zak Collection

(Below) Motor 4446, wearing the more "traditional" E44 garb of road dirt and "white worms", escorts westbound traffic thru the station at Metuchen, N.J.in July 1976, just a year or so before the platforms were raised at this suburban stop by NJ DOT and UMTA funds.

R.J. Yanosey

It's May 17, 1969 at Trenton, N.J., and two ex PRR electric locomotives are performing, as expected, for their still-solvent, new owner, the Penn Central Company. GG-1 4884 (Big Boy ?) raises track dust as she thunders east with a pre Amtrak Florida train as the still-PRR-painted 4457 waits with freight on track 2.

M.S. Zak Collection

R.J. Yanosey

E44's 4458-4465 were rebuilt with silicon diode rectifers, horsepower increased to 5000 and then reclassified E44a. Here, E44a 4460 reaches for the "high wire" while waiting to receive permission from the nearby "WA-5" tower and proceed thru Waverly Yard, Newark, N.J., March 1973. After several years of Conrail service the E44a's were sent to NJ Transit as part of Conrail's disengagement from the commuter business. At NJT they languished for several years never turning a wheel, until finally being sold to Amtrak in 1987 for use as M of W work train power.

89

E33
4600-4610

NH

In the early 1950's the obscure, coal hauling Virginian Railway ordered a dozen 3300 hp ignitron rectifier electric locomotives to replace some antiquated side rodded units that had been in service since the road initiated electric service earlier in the century. After the N&W Railroad absorbed the Virginian in 1959, the electrification of this isolated stretch of track was abandoned in favor of diesels and the surplus electrics were soon sold at bargain prices to the New Haven.

R.J. Yanosey

Herbert H. Harwood

M.S. Zak Collection

(Top) Passed into Penn Central ownership in 1969, 4607 models her 4th owner's name at Kearny, February 1977. Actually, although the photo doesn't show it, the unit had a fifth owner at that time: Conrail.

(Center) Helpers like 4601 were standard for southbound freight trains thru the B&P tunnels in Baltimore because of the grade and curve within. The 4601 provides ample power for this local freight at B&P Jct., in June 1974.

(Left) The 4602 and a fellow "brick" wait patiently for a crew to take the train west along the Trenton Branch and out of Morrisville Yard, Fallsington, Pa., January 25, 1976.

Southbound, along the Northeast Corridor which was now the property of Amtrak, came 4603 (right), now in the employ of Conrail but still painted for PC. In a second the train will pass under the B&O's mainline in this scene at Halethorpe, Md., August 1977.

(Below, center) The 4604 and 4610 bring some empty auto racks and pigs east at Baltimore, Md. in March 1971. The E33's never seemed as dirty as their E44 brethren since they were all given fresh PC black paint in 1969. While passenger GG-1's would receive periodic cleaning at the car wash on the loop at Sunnyside, the freight hood electrics required buckets and mops, a service rarely rendered. Incidentally, the car washer was fine for the sides, but never quite touched the noses above the "hips" of the G's.

Herbert H. Harwood

M.S. Zak Collection

Herbert H. Harwood

A single E33 4605 takes a freight east, past "Morris" tower, Morrisville, Pa., January 30, 1971.

91

D.T. Walker

Webster's Dictionary defines the word "pantograph" as "a mechanical framework of jointed rods . . . an extendible arm." The E33 photos on this page are illustrative of that definition.

(Top) The 4606 has its pan extended to a maximum at "WA-5" tower within Waverly Yard, Newark, N.J., July 17, 1977. Behind the "pan" are visible a diamond shaped "High Wire" sign, along with the ex Lehigh Valley bridge which spanned the PRR at that point. WA-5 governed movements from the Passaic and Harsimus Branch to and from Waverly Yard.

(Left, center) The pans on 4609 are gradually returning to normal height after collapsing somewhat while passing beneath the concrete overpass five cars back in Trenton, N.J., April 11, 1970.

(Left) The pan on 4610 is extended a little more than usual for a train on a mainline as it departs Enola thru Lemoyne, Pa. in May 1969. In the later years of Penn Central, such high wire on secondary and yard tracks could present serious problems. The low joints of badly maintained track could start the unit rocking at certain critical speeds to the point of springing the pantograph out from the wire. Such an occurrence always resulted in serious delays as the pan would rip not only catenary wire down, but also possibly the messenger and clips. Without enough money for proper track maintenance, PC reacted in the only way it could, by lowering both track speed and catenary in such locales.

P2
4622-4642

Since Pennsy was by far, the predominant operator of electric locomotives, the Penn Central numbering system for electric locomotives was built around the larger quantities of that road. NYC and NH electric locomotives were assigned numbers in the 46, 47 and 4900 series.

The ex Cleveland Union Terminal electrics had been classified P-1a's, before the mid-1950's rebuilding. After GE was through with them, the locomotives (now P2's) were equipped for 600 volt d.c. outside third rail and shipped east for Hudson Division service. The first unit finished, #222 was classified P2a. It is viewed at Harmon (right), only several weeks into February 1968 and the Penn Central merger, with an eastbound train from Chicago in tow for GCT. This was the only P2a.

R.J. Yanosey

The more numerous P2b's (20) were for the most part painted PC black and continued to perform their usual chores until the 1969 affiliation with New Haven. P2b 4626 (below) in fresh black awaits the arrival of a southbound train at Harmon in order to relieve the E8's and finish the journey to Grand Central Terminal.

R.J. Yanosey

The FL9's from the New Haven were ideal solutions to the double locomotive requirements of certain commuter trains which ran on former NYC rails and their transfer to these lines resulted in rapid reductions in the P2 fleet. By the early seventies, the only work which belonged to these many wheeled monsters was the long distance trains which still had to switch off from their E8's at Harmon. (Above) A P2b pictured in its natural environ: the caverns of Grand Central Station, November 1972.

Soon, however, as Amtrak also started making use of FL9's and bought third-rail equipped Turbo Trains, the P2's found themselves at the gates of the scrap iron dealer, like 4635, (below) at Naporano Iron & Metal, Newark, N.J., April 1973. Note the Great Northern F7B first up.

R.J. Yanosey

T Motor
4655-4680

"T motor" was a term given to all the electric engines in classes T1a, T1b, T2a, T2b and T3a. These locomotives were the mainstay of the familiar NYC electrification in the New York City area for decades. The T motors were constructed from 1913 thru 1926 and handled much of the NYC's passenger traffic until many were relieved with the arrival of the Cleveland displaced P motors in the 1950's. The surviving T motors were all but eliminated when the FL9 invasion began in 1969.

(Top, right) In a classic example of carrying "upgrading" to new extremes, Penn Central replaced its 1910 built, ex PRR DD-1 with a 1913 built, ex NYC T1b in Sunnyside wire train service. T1b 4655, the ex NYC 255 sits next to a loading dock with ex PRR B-1 4756 and some GG-1's on September 28, 1969.

(Center) Within a year or so, the T1b was itself replaced with the 1926 built, T3a 4678, pictured at SSYD, March 25, 1972. By 1974 standard operating procedure for the wire train was to "borrow" a set of LIRR MU's and the T motors' last job disappeared.

(Bottom) Back in happier days in mainline service in February 1968, an unrenumbered, still NYC painted T motor brings a Poughkeepsie train south through Ossining, N.Y. Ossining is home to the infamous Sing Sing State Prison.

J.W. Swanberg

J.W. Swanberg

R.J. Yanosey

S motors enabled the New York Central Railroad to make the electrification plans of the very early part of the Twentieth Century a reality. Though constantly "bumped" by newer models, the S motors always found work on the busy NYC passenger system. When Penn Central took over, 14 of the aged locomotives could still be found. Although chiefly engaged in switching in the electrified territory, the little S2 still occasionally saw service on live trains.

Rugged little engines, their usefulness and reliability carried some right through Penn Central and into the Conrail era as seen in this photo (left) of S2's 4733 and 4715 alongside FL9 5057 at Harmon shops, December 9, 1976. Imagine, active locomotives which almost spanned the life of the New York Central; the end of the Vanderbilt era to Conrail.

(Below) 4715 pauses from switching a cut of passenger cars to bask in the sun at Harmon, May 1977.

J.W. Swanberg

R. J. Yanosey

The 4723 takes a breather at Harmon on February 28, 1973 (right). When possible it is always optimum to find a locomotive in third rail territory without the third rail and cover boards blocking the running gear. This example is particularly excellent due to the perfect low illumination.

(Below) S2 4733 rests in the Harmon shops, June 1973 looking like it's in a museum. Thankfully, several of these famous locomotives actually have found their way to real museums.

J.W. Swanberg

H.W. Serig, Herbert H. Harwood Collection

B1
4751 - 4757

When PRR was building an electrified empire, the road felt it could afford the luxury and initial cost of building new electric switching locomotives. The 42 B1's built served well at electric terminal areas in the east, but began to suffer as the need for passenger train switching diminished and the more flexible diesel arrived. By the time of Penn Central, PRR had only six B1's remaining, all of which were utilized in the vast passenger yards at Sunnyside, Queens, N.Y. One by one these units started to disappear (4756 went to Strasburg) until by 1975 all were gone.

All -William J. Brennan

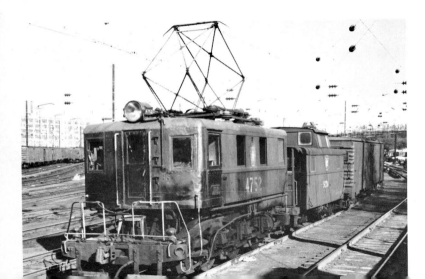

(Top) B1 4751, the last to see service, sits forlornly behind the motor pit at Sunnyside on September 24, 1974.

(Center) Just at merger time, the same 4751 shifts a New Haven "American Flyer" car and a PRR P70, while in the photo at left, the 4752 reaches for the overhead down by the Long Island Railroad's freight yard.

DD1
4780 - 4781

Remarkably, an ancient side-rodded DD1 actually saw service for the Penn Central Railroad. The DD1 was originally designed and built in 1910 to be used as the locomotive to move trains between the then new Pennsylvania Station in New York City, underneath the Hudson River, and over to the Manhattan Transfer in the meadowlands of New Jersey, where the switch to steam was made. This assignment ended in the 1930's when overhead catenary was extended into New York and the DD1's were relegated to more mundane tasks. By 1968 only one DD1 set survived. It was a simple, rugged machine, and despite its advanced age, the third rail equipped electric was used for the very limited run of the nightly wire train in the under river approach tunnels to Penn Station. It is shown at right during its daily all day rest at Sunnyside. Finally in 1969 Penn Central donated the historic piece to Strasburg.

William J. Brennan, RJY Collection

R.J. Yanosey

L6
4790 - 4791

In 1932, somewhat unhappy with the results of its newly constructed P5 electrics and their "Hudson" 4-6-4 wheel arrangement in freight service, Pennsy decided to experiment with a 2-8-2 "Mikado" wheel arrangement. Inexplicably, the new L6's were built equal in weight to the P5's and soon were found too light and low in horsepower to warrant further construction. Two of the three prototypes survived up to the sixties in Penn Station - Sunnyside transfer service.

Renumbered for Penn Central in 1966, L6a 4791 and L6 4790 (right) spent most of 1967 and 1968 "stored serviceable" at the ex PRR yard in Morrisville, Pa., apparently never turning a revenue wheel for their new owner before going to scrap in late '68 or early 1969.

GG1
4800 - 4939

In the middle of the Depression, the Pennsylvania Railroad developed an electric locomotive which will never be surpassed in terms of durability, reliability and good looks: the legendary GG1. Most of the famous GG1 fleet was inherited by successor Penn Central and although averaging about 30 years of age, the units continued their outstanding performance throughout these troubled years.

Quite naturally, the foremost jewel in this electric treasure was "old rivets," # 4800 (right, at Kearny, N.J. 11/74) the first GG1 which lived to see her 40th Anniversary under Penn Central ownership in 1974.

R.J. Yanosey

D.T. Walker

D.T. Walker

Although quite a celebrity to fans and railroaders alike, the 4800 was considered "just another freight G" every work day. In the "with train" views on this page, 4800 is seen leading freights along the Northeast Corridor.

In the southern section of Edison, N.J. (above) on April 5, 1975 she clips along with GG1 4844 which still wears her Pennsy single stripe along with a PC worm.

At left, two months earlier, the weather was considerably less appealing, but "old rivets" proves it is not yet ready for a museum. 4800 and a younger sister await a switch as they sit on the "ought" track leading past the Ford assembly plant, Metuchen, N.J., 2/12/75.

In less than a month, the PC-decaled, PRR-painted, 4840 will become the property of still another railroad. Many of her sisters have already left PC ownership for Amtrak, and some will go to NJ DOT next month, but 4840 and her freight-toting mates will accept the responsibilities of the Consolidated Railroad Company (Conrail). In this shot, (right) 4840 single handedly moves a TV train around a superelevated curve in Metuchen, N.J., March 1976.

D.T. Walker

M.S. Zak Collection

D.T. Walker

PC 4801 (center) has a wonderful touch of class provided by the five stripe scheme which she still proudly bore. Unfortunately, this was the last of the 5-striped G's and would be all black within a year. Shown January 16, 1971 at Morrisville, Pa.

At left, it's the day following that storm that 4800 sat through (opposite page, bottom). As often happens, the storm has cleaned out the atmosphere leaving a brilliant "high" behind. With the sunlight bouncing off the snow to light up undercarriages, and the snow still loose enough to get blown around, wonderful train scenes can be produced, such as this one of 4860 westbound thru Metuchen, N.J., February 13, 1975.

(Top) 4860 wore another unique paint scheme at Morrisville, Pa., August 22, 1971. The unit was later repainted solid black, as seen in the snow scene bottom of page 101.

(Center) The maze of catenary necessary for the switches in the foreground temporarily adds some striping of its own on the 4827 at Baltimore, March 1975. The train is MD-116 passing thru B&P Jct. southbound with some SCL pigs and reefers behind the G.

(Left) The 4870 brings a solid train of hoppers east at Coatesville, Pa. station in June 1972. Coatesville is located on the ex PRR mainline about midway between Paoli and Lancaster, and was the source of much rail traffic from the huge Lukens Steel plant located there.

Eastbound over the wide Bush River near Aberdeen, Md. in October 1974 comes 4804 and 4848 with a long freight. For anyone interested in military transportation, the U.S. Army Ordnance Museum at Aberdeen has a 1 1/2 mile display of such. We'll take the mile or so of railroad transportation on the trestle.

Herbert H. Harwood

Robert Malinoski

D.T. Walker

(Center) One of two very unusual commuter trains in the ex PRR NJ commuter service was train 3845, a 5:25 p.m. NY departure for Trenton. Due to inadequate state financing for more passenger cars, Penn Central showed some good innovation by resurrecting some derelict MP54's, which aside from traction problems, were still intact. With traction provided by a GG1 and an MU pantograph up to provide heat and lights, over 400 more seats were added to the rush hours. PC even made up a similar train set of ex NH MU's for New Brunswick service (3710-3735) which had 3/2 seating. Both trains were known, however, to give quite a "bouncy" ride when the throttle was wound out on the G. In our photo, train 3845's ex PRR MU's behind the 4874 scoot over the "High Line" thru the Jersey Meadows, May 7, 1974 at 5:34 p.m. On the horizon above the GG1, commuters on the Erie Lackawanna ride home in comfort behind a State provided U34CH powered push-pull train.

(Left) In August 1975, the 4881 leads another G and a five car train thru Stelton (Edison), N.J. Two G's on a five car train probably means a ferry move to Wilmington Shops or power balancing.

William J. Brennan

Herbert H. Harwood

(Above) The 4885 brings a Jersey Coast train west on track 4 at Linden, N.J. in September 1968. This Coastline train made stops at Elizabeth and Rahway and hence is not running out on track 2, the normal rush hour track for these trains. At this point, it would seem the PC had enough mainline tracks: B,4,3,2,1, and A; hence, the "Six Roads" nickname at the western end. The overhead bridge is the Staten Island Rapid Transit's freight lifeline into New Jersey and connection with the B&O, CNJ, and LV at Aldene. The PC had a small interchange with SIRT on the other side of the tracks near the bridge abutment.

(Left) The 4881 emerges southbound from the tunnel at the former Pennsylvania Avenue Station in Baltimore, February 1972. This is the western portal of the center tunnel of 3 so-called "B&P Tunnels" on the west side of Baltimore. The portal also originally included a passenger station (which faced the street behind the portal at upper level) and fans to blow out steam locomotive smoke. The passenger station originally served an "uptown" residential area, and was in effect a suburban station.

(Below) The eastbound "Senator" behind GG1 4893 passes a Western Maryland GP9M-F7A powered freight at Bay View, Baltimore, September 1968. Before full Chessie-WM operations integration, the WM used the PRR-PC line from Fulton Jct. in W. Baltimore to Sparrow's Point (Bethlehem Steel).

Herbert H. Harwood

Herbert H. Harwood

In two classic views, the 4894 (above) is taking Florida vacationers home, as the Amtrak train streams across a beautiful old stone viaduct at Beech Street, Wilmington, Delaware in July 1976. Note the unusual extension arms on the catenary pole bottoms. When the viaduct was originally built, evidently no one dreamed of electrification and the need for additional clearance.

(Below) The Raymond Loewy designed 4882 cants to a curve at Bay View, Baltimore and meets one of PC's newest EMD spartan cab designed GP38-2's, the 8158, on a switching run, January 1976.

Herbert H. Harwood

William J. Brennan

On June 8, 1968, the Penn Central was called upon to perform the solemn task of transporting the body of the slain Robert F. Kennedy from NYC to Washington, D.C. Drawing the 21 car cortege were GG1's 4901 and 4903 in appropriate full PC black. Marred by trackside fatalities, the operation was viewed by thousands at trackside and millions more on TV. The funeral train, preceded by a pilot train and followed by protect power (all GG1's) became increasing late due to the crowds surging onto the tracks, and finally arrived in Washington about 4 1/2 hours late.

(Above) At the start of a painful trip, the train already about 1/2 hour late due to the funeral procession from St. Patrick's Cathedral, passes over the Hackensack River via Portal Drawbridge in the Jersey Meadows.

(Center) The rear car, "Philadelphia," bore RFK's remains and is adorned with both laurel and "G" men. Security was attempted, (photographer Brennan was approached by a policeman with gun drawn!) but controlling a hundred thousand or more people spread out along a 225 mile right of way is nearly impossible.

(Bottom) Already 4 hours late the train passes the crowds lined up through Baltimore. In another 40 miles, Penn Central will end its thankless task and RFK will find his final rest near his brother in Arlington National Cemetery.

William J. Brennan

Herbert H. Harwood

The passengers on Train 23 (above) are getting in a little "freight only" mileage, as the train negotiates the Trenton Cut-Off through Woodbourne, Pa., April 25, 1971 due to a wreck blocking the mainline in Philadelphia.

(Right) On May 10, 1869 at Promontory, Utah, the States became truly United as a gold spike was driven to complete the last mile of America's first transcontinental railroad. East coast fans anxious to join the planned festivities for the 100th Anniversary in 1969, assembled a steam drawn "Golden Spike Centennial Limited," whose eastern most leg would be pulled by electric power. PC obliged by painting 4902 in a matching powder blue "American Railroads" scheme. The Penn Central locomotive wore this scheme for some time after the Anniversary before regaining her normal black. The instant notable is shown at Philadelphia (right) and westbound at Trenton, N.J. (below) in the summer of 1969.

(Above) The engineer aboard "red P" 4915 gives a wave to his buddy on the "Reds" (MP54's) making a station stop at Elizabeth, N.J., June 1968. The 4915 is slowing to 55 mph for the pronounced "S" curve thru Elizabeth. GG1's with "red P's" were rarely photographed, since all so adorned were repainted with white lettering within a year.

(Left) The more customary 4937 is passing "Elmora" tower on the extreme opposite end of the same "S" curve at Elizabeth in May 1972.

(Below) Amtrak numbered 916, but still PC painted, the GG1's of this eastbound observe the "double pantograph order" placed in effect during sleet and snow storms, as they pass thru Metuchen, N.J., February 12, 1975.

R.J. Yanosey

E40
4970 - 4977

NH

Besides the E33 ex Virginian rectifiers, Penn Central obtained some other serviceable electric locomotives through its alliance with New Haven in 1969. New Haven 371-377 and 379 were commonly known as "Jets" or "Screaming Eagles" to the NH crews that used them in passenger service (NH officially called them EP5's). By the early 1970's, a lack of proper maintenance by both NH and PC, resulted in E40's that continually were raising havoc with Grand Central rush hours by having road failures and smokey electrical fires at very inopportune times. When the locomotives were finally deemed too unreliable for commuter service, Penn Central elected to try the remaining three units in freight service after some minor rebuilding.

Stripped of one pantograph, the now freight service only 4973 (above) and the 4977 (right) at Kearny, N.J., May 1976.

(Below) The 4973 takes N-13 west through Trenton, N.J., January 31, 1976. N-13 was a local pickup freight that cleaned out yards from Newark, N.J. west, finally terminating at Morrisville, Pa..

R.J. Yanosey

M.S. Zak Collection

Picture yourself as a new rail commuter as the 4973, above, pulls into the station with your first train. It doesn't exactly instill confidence in you that you will arrive at work on time. By early Penn Central, the "Jets" were used on the heaviest New Haven Region commuter trains (above, Stamford, Ct., 11-6-70). When they ran they were very powerful, since experiments showed that even two FL9's couldn't handle the trains and schedules the E40's did. Finally, after one particularly disasterous rush hour caused by

an E40 burning up within the confines of Grand Central Terminal, the units were banished to freight service over on the former PRR.

In the bottom photo, the N-12 is propelled through Trenton, January 18, 1976 behind the power of the same 4973 now exiled to NJ and hiding under a varnish of PC black. The first two TTX flatcars bear auto frames bound for either the Ford plant at Metuchen or GM's at Linden, N.J.

M.S. Zak Collection

After their reworking, the E40's could be found in a number of locations within the electrification, but soon settled down to assignments out of Morrisville, Pa. on eastbound local pickups that would have required two high horsepower diesels.

(Above) The 4977 and train may give the appearance of a short hotshot merchandise train, but this train at Trenton, N.J., January 2, 1976 is actually the A-1 which worked the electrified Jamesburg Branch to Brown's Yard, and now is returning to Morrisville.

(Below) The 4977 gets the eastbound counterpart, A-2, moving from the yards at Morrisville on November 24, 1974.

M.S. Zak Collection

5000 Series: FL9's and Low Horsepower Road Switchers

M. S. Zak collection

R. J. Yanosey

R. J. Yanosey

FL9
5000 - 5059

In the late 1950's, the New Haven, faced with the prospect of buying both new passenger diesels AND electrics, elected to work with GM on a dual mode unit that could operate on the third rail in the NYC electrified zones, and as a pure diesel in the non-electrified territory. If operationally, not all that was promised was delivered, at least the resulting 60 FL9's became instant celebrities for their striking paint schemes and the handsome bulldog noses which most fans had thought would never be built again.

Under Penn Central ownership, three paint schemes would be associated with the units:

(Top) "Class" locomotive 5000 is regaled in the full PC black paint scheme as it awaits shipment east from Enola, May 30, 1970 after having had a ten year overhaul. Note the rare B-C wheel arrangement.

(Center) More common, until the MTA scheme, was this "interim" PC decaling and renumbering as shown at Brewster, N.Y., September 1974. Note that "blotch" under the number board of 5030. That's one way "car knockers" earn their nickname. NH Region car inspectors routinely would bang the locomotive in this spot with their hammer when signalling the engine crew that their intended work was completed.

(Bottom) When the NY State Metropolitan Transit Authority got more involved with their passenger service after the bankruptcy, its objections to PC black resulted in this blue and yellow scheme pictured on 5038 at Brewster, May 1976.

At New Haven, May 1971, ex NH power congregates in several PC paint schemes.

H. A. Smith, Herbert H. Harwood Collection

Given the choice of the expedient NH-PC interim scheme or a faded modernistic MTA paint job, the PC black design, slightly weathered, looked pretty good, as in this shot of 5022 on #914 from Brewster at 125th Street, NYC, April 20, 1971.

J.W. Swanberg

J.W. Swanberg

The 5030 and 5040 on #895 for Poughkeepsie accelerate out of Harmon, August 5, 1975. The bottom five side panels on 5030 are replacement MTA blue fiberglass.

The former NYC Harlem Division was a natural place to utilize the FL9's talents since the third rail electrification from GCT only extended as far as North White Plains, N.Y. and much of the commuter traffic extended north another 23 miles to Brewster.

(Top) Due to a shortage of FL9's at Brewster, train 948 was operating south with former NYC RS3 5500 when it died enroute. FL9's 5048-5007, the intended switch-off power at North White Plains anyway, were sent north to couple and tow everything in. NWP, July 28, 1977.

(Center) The first day with MTA cars and the new livery on the 5050 - 5014 brings some cheer to the commuters on train 912 at Brewster, July 29, 1970.

(Bottom) To the west, along the aptly named Hudson Division above Peekskill, N.Y., FL9's 5047 and 5053 are in charge of train 8836 from Poughkeepsie on June 20, 1976.

All-J.W. Swanberg

H16-44
5100 - 5174

M.S. Zak Collection

M.S. Zak Collection

J.W. Swanberg

In the early 1950's both PRR and NYC purchased some of Fairbanks Morse's Loewy styled H16-44's. The unit was firmly on the fast track to extinction on these roads when Penn Central was formed in 1968. While the NYC units did see some service they were never given PC decals or paint. The sole PRR survivor, 5158, is shown at top in PC service at Chicago, August 11, 1968. It was the only PRR or NYC H16-44 to receive a full PC repaint job.

In the center photo one full year later, August 24, 1969 at Chicago, the celebrated, now fully PC'd 5158, shares a weed infested engine facility with an Alco Century 636 demonstrator and a younger ex NH version of the H16-44. The 5158 was also unique in having the only known case of "slanted" numbers under its windows.

(Left) After the passage of still another year, 5158 finds her short claim to fame over with and sits amidst equally ill-fated Baldwin and E7 brethren at the East Altoona deadline 9/13/70.

After the 1969 New Haven inclusion, Penn Central shipped that road's 15 later styled H16-44's to its Chicago terminal, where all remaining ex NYC-PRR FM's were based to provide easier geographic access to the FM parts supply in Beloit, Wisconsin. These units were the final car body design of the H16-44: the boxy Train Master look, as opposed to the earlier NYC and PRR Loewy styled varieties (NH also had 10 of the earlier variety which came very close to making the PC roster, seeing service in NH's Bronx terminal during 1967 and '68. One older NH H16-44, the 593, even lasted in the Altoona scrapline until 1971).

Above, the 5161 displays her short and long hoods at Chicago 8-9-70 (top) and 5-23-69 (center). (Left) The 5174, last in the series, has only an interim scheme to wear at Chicago, August 3, 1969.

RS2
5207 - 5229

Five New York Central RS2's made it into Penn Central. The 1500 hp predecessor to the RS3 was constructed in the late '40's and is quickly distinguished from the RS3 by the lack of a battery box on the running board behind the cab.

(Right) RS2 5229, the former NYC 8229, works a Pittsfield - Canaan way freight at Canaan, Ct., in October 1974. This is the same unit seen in road service, spliced between FA's on page 17.

Jack Armstrong, Herbert H. Harwood Collection

Herbert H. Harwood

Herbert H. Harwood

RS3m
5227 - 5477

In early 1972, Penn Central came to task with the reality that it had a desperate need for some more reliable secondary power. Unable to commit brand new power to these roles and already rebuilding early EMD switchers, PC turned to its large fleet of non EMD diesels. Not wishing to prolong the Alco - Baldwin legacy, however, PC was reluctant to rebuild these units in kind when their manufacturers were out of business, parts were more difficult to stock, and the move to EMD, GE standardization was an accepted fact. The railroad solved part of its problem by electing to rebuild some of its Alco RS3 fleet with EMD prime movers removed from surplus E8's. Ex New Haven RS3 m, was elected as the guinea pig in April 1972 and emerged at the end of that year from Altoona as the "no nose" 5477 (above left, at Bay View, Baltimore, March 1973). After testing for six months, Penn Central made another try which resulted in 5230 (ex NYC 8230), becoming the next 1200 hp RS3M, but this time with a "low nose" (Baltimore, 9/73, left). Sufficiently pleased, PC began a small program to create more of these units, and assigned numbers in one block in the 9950 series which are examined more closely on pages 227 - 229.

R. J. Yanosey

Herbert H. Harwood, RJY Collection

E. D. Galvin, Herbert H. Harwood Collection

Herbert H. Harwood, RJY Collection

RS3
5203 - 5598

The Penn Central inherited a goodly number of RS3's from its three predecessors who had purchased the units extensively during the early 50's. Numbered from the 5200's to the 5500's, PC used these 1600 hp Roadswitchers for transfer, switching and local freight duties, and several even stayed in Harlem Division passenger service. Coming from three roads which utilized the talented Alcos in various assignments, it is natural that the PC RS3 fleet has a number of interesting variations.

(Top) RS3 5316 is the ex NYC 8316 and carries an air reservoir tank atop its long hood; a feature only seen on PC on some ex NYC units. Once a passenger locomotive, by 1974 the steam generator had been removed and a block of concrete substituted; in addition, the s/g water tank was converted to an additional fuel tank. Shown at Kearny, N.J. one month before Conrail.

(2nd from top) The 5416 is the ex PRR 8436 as evidenced by her PRR style large number boards. Ex PRR RS3's could be found both with and without the special number boards. Shown at Baltimore, August 1974.

(3rd from top) The 5480 is more or less a stock RS3 still in NH colors but lacking her NH 545 number and carrying the PC decals of her new owner, at Framingham, Mass., April 1971.

(Bottom) The 5506 was once NYC 8264, an RS3 with a steam generator for passenger service, as evidenced by the stack coming out of the top of the short hood. At this time (November 1974) her duties were the less glamorous switching of freight cars at Bay View Yard, Baltimore.

RDC's were especially prone to problems during snowfalls. Aside from their known tendency to improperly "shunt" the signal system, the RDC's could and would derail at grade crossings as plowed snow froze hard into banks and "lifted" the lightweight car off the rail. Consequently, the New Haven Region routinely placed road-switchers, such as 5481 (above) at Danbury, Ct., January 4, 1970, ahead of RDC's in such situations.

(Left) Honorary steam engine 5509 gets the normally FL9 propelled train 897 for Poughkeepsie underway at Harmon on August 23, 1973.

(Below) RS3 5567 mu'd with another ex PRR Alco, DL702 6865 (with a "red P"), pumps the air up on a Sparrows Point transfer at Bay View Yard, Baltimore, December 1971.

M. S. Zak Collection

Herbert H. Harwood, RJY Collection

J. W. Swanberg

When 97% owned Lehigh Valley needed more available power, Penn Central decided to do a little creative swapping with its stepchild. PC sent LV some serviceable RS3's while PC used the derelict LV units as trade ins at GE. (Above) The RS3 which had seen service on the Valley for 20 years as Lehigh Valley 212, now assumes the identity of Penn Central 5401 (2nd) and fulfills a short-lived sacrificial role for her new owner at GE's Erie, Pa. plant on March 12, 1971. PC 5401 (1st) would live on another 6 years as LV 212 (2nd).

(Left) Power for the Delmarva penninsula: RS3's 5567, 5555, and 5511 lay over at Delmar, Delaware on July 22, 1972. Ex PRR, PRR and NYC, respectively.

(Below) The 5578 heads an interesting RS3-DL701-GP9B-RS3 combo powering a coal train transfer through a tie butt littered portion of Baltimore in June 1974. It used to be that the railroads could find ready markets for their full length used ties, as landscaping and earth retaining walls. With the development of mechanized tie removal systems that saved the railroad labor costs but also sawed the tie into three pieces, the troublesome problem of tie butt disposal arose. What do you do with a million chunks of wood that can't be burned (smokey creosote) and can't be buried (carcinogens)?

GP7
5600 - 5959

RJY Collection

The very popular GP7 produced sales for EMD from both Pennsy and the Central circa 1951. This market was tempered, however, by the then popular belief that the general purpose GP7 was just that: a jack of all trades, while the mainline belonged to the cab unit. By the time the GP9 was introduced, however, this philosophy was dead. Nevertheless, the GP7's on both PRR and NYC had started life for special assignments, sometimes off the main, and continued that right on through their PC tenure.

When the Penn Central assembled these 1500 hp EMD's under one banner, differences abounded, even among ex NYC GP7's:

(At the top) 5633, the ex NYC unit of the same number, is a plain vanilla GP7 shown at Bay City, Mich., May 20, 1972.

(2nd from top) The bland, ex NYC 5639's singular point of interest is her road number, still in NYC positioning at West Springfield, Mass., April 1974.

(3rd from top) The ex NYC 5825 is a GMDL (Canadian) GP7 purchased secondhand from C&O (ex C&O 5727) shown at Windsor, Ontario, August 1972. Customs tax kept the GMDL GP7's and 9's captive on the Canada Southern portion of the PC.

(Bottom) Former NYC now PC subsidiary, Peoria & Eastern's GP7's were also given PC logos and a spot on the roster. 5618 is shown at Wood River, Ill. in June 1977. The little P&E would also gain "fallen flag" status because of Conrail.

Jack Armstrong, Herbert H. Harwood Collection

D. Hamley, Herbert H. Harwood Collection

William A. Raia, Herbert H. Harwood Collection

121

M. S. Zak Collection

(Above) Amazingly, GP7 5954 still has a roofline induction radio antenna at Conway on April 6, 1968 to give away her PRR heritage despite the fact that Pennsy had abandoned the system some 4 years earlier. Note the lack of a dynamic brake. Pennsy and the Central purchased both equipped and non equipped GP7's, so a dynamic brake or the lack of it is not useful in distinguishing PC GP7's.

(Below) The 1500 hp of GP7 5607 (ex NYC) shuffles some empty Amtrak cars out of Union Station, Chicago and out to the coach yard in May, 1976.

J.R. Quinn, Herbert H. Harwood Collection

J.W. Swanberg

(Above) Emerging from the Detroit River tunnels in a burst of diesel exhaust, PC GP7 5671 and still PRR, GP9 7103 fight hard to pull their train up the steep incline and into the station area of Detroit on August 30, 1969. This "Windsor Puller" is still mostly under the Detroit River which connects Lake Erie with Lake Huron (with Lake St. Clair in between).

(Below) The 5872 has 4 gons of ties from a creosoting plant in Mifflin and some other local freight in hand as the train moves past "Lewis" tower in Lewistown, Pa., August 1976. Prior to 1928 the tower was known as "RW" when everything was done telegraphically, but aside from minor changes (the brick shingle siding for one), it remains as constructed in 1914. "Lewis" would vanish about 10 years later, after almost 72 years of service, as Conrail completed its track reduction and CTC projects on the ex PRR Middle Division.

R. J. Yanosey

R. J. Yanosey

Two examples of dynamic brake equipped, ex PRR GP7's are demonstrating the varied assignments of this versatile unit in May 1975 in central Pennsylvania.

(Top) The 5874 enters the yard at Lewistown, Pa. with a local freight off the old Sunbury & Lewistown Ry. This innocuous branch, once extending all the way to Sunbury, Pa., has the distinction of being the test site for PRR's locomotive cab signal system many years ago. Under Penn Central it was dubbed the Milroy Industrial Track and restricted to 15 mph or less.

(Below) Sister 5876 has a work train out on westbound track 3 picking up tie butts at Ardenheim, just east of Huntington, Pa. To the right in this photo is Route 22, one of the original principal highways through Pennsylvania. Both Route 22 and the ex PRR mainline parallel each other from Harrisburg to Pittsburgh, sometimes fighting for room in the Juniata Valley, sometimes miles apart. The Pennsy was there first, but the highway received abundant superior alignment when it occupied much of the State Canal's old right of way which had been abandoned after PRR became successful.

R. J. Yanosey

Robert Malinoski

(Above) The merger is only 20 days old for the New Haven and already evidence is invading Maybrook, N.Y., the traditional New England freight gateway. Within two years Penn Central would all but close this facility, but you can't tell from this array of power on Monday, January 20, 1969.

(Below) Having gingerly completed the 12 mile downhill run from Gallitzin, U25C 6507 and mates pass Altoona Station in July 1968 and enter the yard for a new crew.

William J. Brennan, RJY Collection

William J. Brennan, RJY Collection

(Above) The only HH660 on the Penn Central roster was the ex New Haven 0924. The HH660 (High Hood 660 hp) was produced by Alco 1939-1940 and equipped with a 539 (May 1939) engine. PC 9411 just wouldn't quit, so stayed on the roster until 1971. Shown here at Dover Street, So. Boston, in September 1969.

(Below) The year 1970 was disasterous for the Penn Central but you couldn't tell from this freight at Jersey City in January, led by the "red P" 2232. This was a PC transfer to the Jersey Central via the National Docks Branch. In years past, such a transfer would have entered the CNJ's Communipaw Yard at Phillips Street, but since passenger service to Jersey City was ended as a result of the Aldene Plan (1967), this one occupies the abandoned passenger terminal's eastbound main.

R. J. Yanosey

Robert Malinoski

(Above) TT-8 was usually the first eastbound piggyback train past the Horseshoe Curve every afternoon. Helper Century 628 6307 leads the road power 6093 & 6097 (SD40's) and 18 piggybacks, 7 boxcars, 27 livestock 7 more piggybacks plus caboose 21343 at 5:36 p.m. 10/1/1968.

(Below) After serving Penn Central for several years in local freight service in the Boston area, ex NH FA1 1331 was sent to Altoona in June 1971 for storage. After 9 months there, the Alco made her last trip, up to Collinwood where the unit was photographed, awaiting stripping in March 1972.

RJY Collection

(Above) On a fine day in May 1969, westbound hoppers leave Enola behind a GP35 still in full PRR, a GP30 in "red P" regalia, and a new U33B in the conventional PC scheme.

(Below) Another interesting combination, just a few miles north on September 8, 1968, is underway with a trainload of covered, coil steel gondolas. Power is provided by PRR SD45 6196, PC DL600B 6814, and PRR RS3 5420. A very unusual combination for a mainline freight, but apparently all three units are working as evidenced by the exhausts.

R. J. Yanosey

(Above) A pair of GP38's (above) cruise down the ex PRR four track main in the beautiful Juniata River Valley of Central Pennsylvania. The train is passing a standard PRR station at Mifflin, Pa. in this August 1976 scene. Mifflin is named after former governor Thomas Mifflin, delegate and signer to the Constitution (1787) despite an unpopular attempt in 1777 to oust George Washington as Commander of the Continental Army.

(Below) SE-2 was a run through train from the Rock Island at Silvis Ill. to Elkhart, Ind. with pooled RI-PC power. In this photo RI 165 leads PC passenger F7B's 4159 and 4158 still in PRR, and PC FP7A 4353 with a 116 car train and RI caboose 17087 at 12:42 p.m. Wednesday, May 8, 1968.

Robert Malinoski

R.J. Yanosey

(Above) In May 1968, F7 1707 sits awaiting sanding at the small engine terminal outside Toledo Union Station. The fresh paint on 1707 is covered by only about the same amount of dust as on the windshields.

(Below) WD-5, with the 1688 heading a F7-GP9-F7-F7-GP20-DL721-RS3 brace, departs the former NYC Weehawken, N.J. yard with 112 cars on Tuesday, April 18, 1968. Today, all the tracks in this scene are gone.

Robert Malinoski

John F. Dalton III, RJY Collection

(Above) Called an EP-5 on the former New Haven, but now classed E40, black 4973 gets the A-1 underway at Brown's Yard, located on the Amboy Secondary Track, Old Bridge, N.J., March 27, 1976. Brown's received traffic from the Freehold and Hightstown Secondary Tracks as well as the Jamesburg Branch which connected with the former PRR mainline at "Midway," Monmouth Jct., N.J..

(Below) The CSB symbol on the PRR stood for Chicago, St. Louis and Boston. Such trains used the PRR east to Altoona and Tyrone, then up the Bald Eagle branch to Lock Haven, the Buffalo - Harrisburg line to Sunbury and then up the branch to the Buttonwood and Hudson yards in the Wilkes-Barre area for D&H - B&M connecting trains. Westbound equivalent CSB-7 has the 6311 - 6063 with 102 cars about 1 mile west of the curve on October 1, 1968.

Robert Malinoski

(Above) A dash of color was added to the black Penn Central landscape when PC bought 10 D&RGW F7's for trade in value and, instead, wound up using 4 of the cabs in freight service until Conrail. Perhaps not believing the units would last, the F's initially had only the "5" taken off their DRGW numbers. PC 721, ex D&RGW 5721 idles in Cleveland, March 1972.

(Below) A little over 1 year old GP38 7727 and a U boat companion are winding down the curving Kiskiminetas River Valley through "Jones' Cut" and into the borough of East Vandergrift, Pa. on a bitter cold February day in 1971. These early GP38's came with the then conventional oil-bath air filters. Beginning with 7738, new GP38's were delivered with the improved "paper air filters."

R. J. Yanosey

(Above)The MTA instigated FL9 paint scheme didn't look bad when the enamel was fresh. Unfortunately, the yellow tended to fade badly and quickly into a rather pale pastel. In this photo, the 5041 is in crisp paint at Brewster, N.Y., 5/75.

(Below) Although this book deals solely with PC diesels and electrics, honorary mention must be given to the "Roger Williams" RDC units with diesel faces. In this dramatic night shot, the Budd-built #140 shares the Boston engine terminal with invading ex PRR E8's, September 1969.

William J. Brennan, RJY Collection

R. J. Yanosey

(Above) In October 1968, Penn Central had a group of new GP40's delivered with an "orange C" rather than the "red P," in what some regarded as a nod to the Central interests or an experiment to see which version was more palatable. Eventually, both versions were dropped in favor of the all-white logo. As example, 3175 shown at Kearny, N.J. in March 1971.

(Below) Both the B1 and the REA refrigerator it tows don't have much of a future in this March 1968, Sunnyside, N.Y. photo. Sunnyside, "Largest Passenger Train Yard in the World," was a "natural" for the use of the scarce electric switchers.

William J. Brennan, RJY Collection

William J. Brennan

(Above) More celebrated later on in life as Lehigh Valley 211, this unique, high nosed RS3 was first PRR, then PC property. "Hammerhead" 5569 would not see PC paint, however, before going over to the Valley in a swap. Here the beetle browed Penn Central Alco is pictured at Providence, R.I. in September 1969.

Robert J. Malinoski

(Below) A high & wide extra west had just FP7 4371 with 2 empty idlers surrounding the loaded generator plus NYC caboose 21771 by "MG" tower west of Horseshoe Curve at 2:05 p.m. on Tuesday, October 1, 1968. MG stood for Mid Grade; (about 1/2 way up the 12 mile climb from Altoona to Gallitzin).

Mark Branibar Collection

(Above) Another colorful Penn Central diesel resulted, when ex NYC subsidiary Merchants Despatch Shops decided to add a little extra splash to their captive shop switcher SW8 #15. The little EMD soon lost its celebrity status, however, when shifted to within the PC fleet proper and repainted full black PC 8605. Shown 1/10/71 at Youngstown, Ohio.

(Below) PC 1501 an ex PRR F7 waits for yet another call to duty at the Collinwood engine terminal, just east of Cleveland on March 9, 1975. 1501 won the tontine by surviving longer than any other PRR freight cab, actually seeing some Conrail service (but not blue paint).

Mark Branibar Collection

6000 Series: Six Axle Diesels

SD35
6000 - 6039

On the Penn Central, the 6000 series meant six axled diesel and this in turn meant Pennsy. The 6000 series contains no ex NH or NYC diesels for the simple reason that neither road ever purchased a six axle diesel.

Long thought of as simply transfer or very heavy yard diesels as the "Special Duty" tag applied to them by EMD implied, PRR had purchased a smattering of SD7's and 9's for just such purposes. When it was shown in the early swing to second generation power that the high horsepower B-B lost much of its advantages in the mountains, PRR decided to test the builder's new claims about high horsepower C-C's and sampled the wares of all three manufacturers. EMD's entry was the C-C version of the GP35, the 2500 hp SD35, manufactured from June of 1964 to January 1966. Among the 40 SD35's ordered, was 6029 shown in PC paint (right) at Kearny, N.J. in March 1976, and 6009 (below) leading tonnage by Kittanning Point, Horseshoe Curve, July 1968. The color of the tracks tell you which way the battle wages here; the two tracks at right being white with the sand of countless upgrade locomotives.

William J. Brennan

R. J. Yanosey

Although liable to pop up anywhere on the mainlines of the Penn Central System, the SD35's were most frequently found in the territories around the Alleghenies they were born to fight. At right, in August 1976 the 6013 has almost put the Middle Division behind it as it passes thru Tyrone, Pa. westbound, the last town of any size before Altoona and the mountain.

R.J. Yanosey

R.J. Yanosey

(Center) CG-8 on the Chicago Greenville, N.J. run with float connections in New York Harbor was always a hot perishable train. The 125 cars on this trip were heavy enough to require 4 units; SD35 6025, SD40 6097, U25B 2513 and GP9 7355 alongside the broad Susquehanna River at "Banks" tower October 1, 1972. There were only 19 perishables on this trip, however, somewhat predicting the future change of "The Ace," CG-8, to a Chicago - Enola hotshot later in Penn Central, as the NY float traffic diminished.

(Bottom) SD35 6028 halts its train in front of venerable "Rockville" tower (in service July 14, 1898) which guards the eastern side of the bridge of the same name, May 1975. Eastbound piggyback trains would usually turn left at Rockville instead of taking the normal freight routing thru Enola Yard. Relayed like the passenger trains, PC took alot of care with its piggyback traffic, recognizing it as being one of railroading's true growth areas in the 70's.

RJY Collection

M. S. Zak Collection

SD40
6040 - 6104
6240 - 6284

The SD40 was first advertised in conjunction with EMD's 1966 645 engine introduction, which also brought forth the GP40 and SD45. Pennsy liked the unit from the start and all 65 SD40's numbered 6040-6104 are ex PRR. The popularity of this diesel continued right into Penn Central, which purchased another 45 in early 1971 and numbered them 6240-6284. Like the earlier SD35's, the SD40's also tended to be found mostly on the mountainous ex PRR lines where their extra tractive effort could be put to best use. They were good system power however, and virtually any mainline train could draw the versatile EMD.

(Top) 6072 in PC paint at Cleveland, April 1972 was an ex PRR unit. Note the SD45 still in PRR at this late date!

(Center) 6277, one of the SD40's purchased new by PC, is shown at Enola, July 1, 1973. Looks like the caustic cleaner that PC used was not properly rinsed off causing this unit's discoloration.

(Below) SD40 6047 and three other EMD's are cresting the Alleghenies just above Gallitzin at "UN," August 1976. "UN" is a remote interlocking where a switch leads pusher locomotives to a turning loop to "AR" tower and eastbound to Altoona.

R. J. Yanosey

It's August 1976. SD40 6042 (left) is now a decade old and awaits the interim paint scheme of her third owner as worn by her coupled mate SD40 6248. The job is one she has performed many times before, however, serving as a "snapper" (pusher) and now making a reverse move at "MO" tower, Cresson, Pa., in order to return east for more work.

R. J. Yanosey

Elmer Treloar, Herbert H. Harwood Collection

R. J. Yanosey

(Center) Penn Central was an integral part of the assembly lines of all three major automobile manufacturers. With close to 30 large car plants on line, PC's traffic (and fortunes) ebbed and flowed with car sales. Undoubtedly, the transportation of new autos and their parts was PC's most valuable traffic: example, 6067 and an SD45 leads rack cars full of Detroit-made automobiles southbound across the DT&I at Dearborn, Mi., June 1972.

(Right) The 6069 with SD45-SD40 help sails downgrade and westward off the Alleghenies at Bradenville, Pa., October 1975.

(Right) The morning rush hour is over now, so SD40 6092 and U25C 6518 can get their train moving again after having been tucked away in the Metuchen yard for an hour or so in August 1976 watching Jersey Arrows shoot by. The train is still mostly in the yard but the two locomotives are making a move off track 1, the eastbound track for NJ DOT locals, to the middle and track 2, for the 13.8 miles from "Lincoln" tower in Metuchen to "Lane" in Newark where the freight can leave the busy Northeast Corridor for the safety of the North Jersey freight yards.

(Below) On "the mountain," "red P" SD40 6070 and a PRR SD45 give a boost to a freight drawing a PRR N8 "cabin" painted focal orange, May 4, 1969.

D. T. Walker

M. S. Zak Collection

At one time the Pennsylvania Railroad employed over 100 towers on its mainline between New York and Chicago to handle the tremendous traffic the railroad bore. Continual signal work and track reduction have made all but a handful a memory. Two examples not typical of standard PRR construction stood within a few miles of each other high in the mountains of western Pennsylvania. At right, SD40 6072 (the very first unit to be painted PC) drops downgrade and assists in dynamic braking as it passes the relatively new "MG" tower east of Gallitzin, Pa. in May 1975. "MG" was constructed in World War II during the crush of wartime traffic to add still more fluidity to the "mountain." It was normally a "part time" tower during PC's tenancy, opening only during summer construction times or in case of a derailment or other track closure. At other times the tracks were straight railed, signals set to automatically clear up, and the tower closed.

R. J. Yanosey

R. J. Yanosey

D. T. Walker

In the center photo above, SD40 pushers 6076 and 6069 return to the base of the mountain at Altoona and are passing by "AR" another "non standard" ex PRR tower located at the crest in Gallitzin, Pa., August 1976.

The Amtrak takeover of passenger stations and an extensive urban redevelopment program at Altoona, Pa. in the mid 70's spelled the doom of the large ex PRR station there. Here (left) SD40 6082 and SD45 6211 westbound pass the Altoona "temporary station" and an otherwise greatly changed horizon on October 10, 1976.

D. T. Walker

(Above) SD40 6076 leads mixed ex NYC and ex PRR GP35's west through Metuchen, N.J. 15 days after Conrail start up, April 15, 1976. Part of the legislation enabling Conrail and Amtrak's NEC takeover, required freights to leave the corridor as soon as possible. At this early date, however, nothing much has changed.

(Below) The ex PRR main line on one side and Route 22 on the other side of the Juniata River, all between two mountains forms the short but scenic "Jacks Narrows" just west of Mr. Union, Pa. In an unusual move, the operator at the appropriately named "Jacks" tower has crossed over train FP-5 from track 3 to 4 to 2. PRR numbered their tracks from the south 1,2,3,4. The 6187, a less than a year old SD40, is assisted by U28C 6523 in hauling this 117 car freight composed of mostly empty reefers on Friday, October 15, 1971.

Robert Malinoski

(OPPOSITE PAGE) PC SD40 6244 and an SD45 companion slip into the east portal at Gallitzin, August 1976. This tunnel is the oldest, having been constructed for the New Portage Railroad in 1850. Almost one hundred years later during the peak of WW II this same bore would see the passage of over 5000 cars a day. It is still in use under Conrail ownership today. (R.J. Yanosey)

R. J. Yanosey

R. J. Yanosey

Robert Malinoski

(This page - top) Three SD40's, bought new in 1971, ascend the mountain near Allegrippus, between the curve and Gallitzin, May 1975. Allegrippus got its name when the brand new steam locomotive of the same name was wrecked here in early 1854. Thereafter, as a memorial, Pennsy crews always referred to this location by that name.

(Center)SD40 6252 and an SD45 have a westbound in tow at Donohoe, Pa., October 1975. Donohoe is located just west of Latrobe, Pa. on the ex PRR main.

(Left) CG-2 with a late morning Chicago departure enroute to Greenville, N.J. is approaching the Grand Trunk Western crossing a few miles west of Valparaiso, Ind.

145

SD45
6105 - 6239

R. J. Yanosey

The V-20, 3600 hp SD45, introduced in 1966 by EMD, was an exciting new idea which many railroads, including the PRR, decided to try. Big, brawny, lots of horsepower, yet equipped with sure footed C-C paws, the SD45 rode a crest of enthusiasm in the mid to late sixties. Pennsy, in fact, purchased a whopping 130 units, completely overwhelming the 5 SD45's later purchased by successor Penn Central.

(Above, left) PC 6183 at Cresson in August 1976 is a sample of an ex PRR SD45.

(Center, left) 6238 at Camden, N.J., July 26, 1969, is a comparatively rare, PC purchased SD45.

(Below) Two SD45's headed by the 6134 start down "The Slide" east of Gallitzin, July 1973. "The Slide" is the one mile straightaway that is a 2.27% downgrade a few miles above the Curve. Freights must be down to 12 mph here in order to have their trains fully under control.

M. S. Zak Collection

R. J. Yanosey

(Right)The 4600 hp combination of an SD40 and SD45 seemed popular with Penn Central and was found on many trains in ex PRR territory. SD45 6141 leads an SD40 and a TV train eastward under signal bridge 310 (miles from Philadelphia) and up the .94% grade at Bradenville, Pa. in October 1975.

(Below, center) PC 6143 and fellow SD45 parallel another westbound freight through downtown Altoona, Pa., on May 4, 1969. This is approximately the same angle in the "redevelopment" photo, bottom of page 142, but 6 1/2 years earlier.

(Bottom) Three SD45's and their eastbound freight are silhouetted on the graceful stone arches of Rockville Bridge on April 21, 1976. The 48 span bridge is 3,810 feet long and carries 4 tracks across the wide Susquehanna River. It was completed in 1902.

R. J. Yanosey

M. S. Zak Collection

D. T. Walker

The angular radiators and straight lines of the long hood of SD45 6150 contrast nicely with the circular lines of the bore it is about to enter. The big EMD (left) leads eastbound piggyback traffic into the New Portage tunnel at Gallitzin, August 1976.

(Below) Two SD45's and a Century 636 attempt to defy the laws of nature by holding back a fully loaded coal train coming down 12 miles of 1+% grade. With blue brakeshoe smoke covering the hoppers, PC (PRR) SD45 6146 passes "Alto" tower and safely enters Altoona in August 1968.

R. J. Yanosey

William J. Brennan

The little town of Spruce Creek, Pennsylvania is nestled in the mountains on the ex PRR mainline between Tyrone and Huntingdon (east of Altoona, for those unfamiliar with Pennsylvania). At this point the PRR was forced to bore two tunnels to maintain the easy gradients of the Middle Division. In the photo below, Penn Central SD45 6209 blasts out of the Spruce Creek tunnel with a westbound and a haze of exhaust smoke in August 1976. Two months later and about 1 mile west of the tunnel a SD45-SD40 combo (right) headed by 6174 accelerates out of "Spruce" interlocking with a TV (Trailvan) train.

D. T. Walker

R. J. Yanosey

(Left) Penn Central SD45's 6208 and 6125 ride a freight downhill east of Gallitzin in May 1975, helping the road locomotives with their dynamic braking. 6208 and most of the other Penn Central SD45's were sold to the Chicago & Northwestern for coal service in 1984.

(Below, center) In May 1968, PC (PRR) SD45 6225 is assisted by a PRR GP35 and a NYC U boat on a transfer at 75th and Western, in Chicago.

(Bottom) 6237, one of the SD45's purchased new by Penn Central in August 1968, crosses over in front of "Gray" tower located in Tyrone, Pa., August 1976. PC purchased only 5 of the SD45's in 1968, probably because the more expensive maintenance costs of a 20 cylinder engine were becoming more apparent. Only a few years later, sales of EMD V-20's would all but vanish.

R. J. Yanosey

R. J. Yanosey

R. J. Yanosey

C628
6300 - 6314

Beginning in December 1963, Alco introduced its C-C, high horsepower hood entrant into the second generation diesel race; the 2750 hp, Century 628. PRR purchased 15 of the 251C engined locomotives, which PC later inherited.

Ronald Amberger, RJY Collection

Ronald Amberger, RJY Collection

R. J. Yanosey

PC 6301 at Wilmerding (top, 2-73), 6302-6304 at Pitcairn, Pa. (center, 2-73), and 6311 at Pitcairn (left, 10-75) are examples of several different PC paint schemes for their Century 628's. The fame of the Altoona-Cresson pusher activities have all but obliterated the fact that there were other pusher efforts conducted by Penn Central. For instance, from Pitcairn, Pa. (just east of Pittsburgh) there is about a 1% grade for eastbounds for 30 miles until Derry, Pa. Loaded coal trains and some other heavy freights required assistance here in order not to tie up the railroad, so early in 1970 PC decided to base most of its C628's at Pitcairn for pusher service. The big Alcos were used alone or with a fellow C628; on the rear, or on the head end as in the color shot on page 127.

ALCO

(Above) Century 628 6309 and two ex PRR GP9's have eastbound coal moving at a good clip through "View" interlocking, Duncannon, Pa., May 29, 1971.

(Left) 6311 awaits her next pusher assignment, Pitcairn, October 1975.

(Below) This photograph probably best illustrates how wishful thinking can become reality. Imagine the photographer's delight to see "red P" 6304 leading an Alco Century 636 demonstrator as it came into his viewfinder. He clicks the shutter, and hopes that everything will turn out all right. It did, as evidenced by this fine photograph taken at "View," July 13, 1969.

C630
6315 - 6329

In mid 1965, Alco introduced its 251E powered, Century 630. Distinguishable from the C628 by the large aftercooler bulge on the long hood, the C630 produced 3000 hp. Ever faithful, Pennsy signed up for another 15 big Centuries.

At right, it may be 9 months into the merger and former PRR C630 6318 may be in Penn Central paint, but the sign above states "New York Central Weehawken Engine Terminal" in October 1968.

(Below) Sister 6322 was still not painted PC when it helped a freight through Baltimore in July of the following year. Full repainting depended on many vageries, causing some diesels in a class to be done rather quickly; others never receiving any attention for years.

R. J. Yanosey

Herbert H. Harwood, RJY Collection

William J. Brennan, RJY Collection

C630 6323 led an interesting and varied career judging by these photos. (Above) The big Alco still in as delivered PRR paint, assaults "the mountain" together with new found partner NYC's GP40 3011, at "Benny" just below Gallitzin in August 1968. Within a year Penn Central would deem the big Alcos not as reliable as comparable GM and GE power, take them off the road freights and assign them to pusher and Mingo Jct service where they could cause less damage. As the curtain closed on Penn Central, the now PC'd 6323 found itself in an Alco reunion conducted at Mingo Jct., Ohio by new owner, Conrail. Below, 6323 shares company with a Lehigh Valley C628 and two EMD's on a Mingo bound freight, just after Conrail's startup.

D. Hamley, RJY Collection

William J. Brennan

Alco had put 3000 hp into its Century 630's but still wasn't able to gain entry into the rosters of many roads. Loyal PRR continued to try to buy Alco products but persistent problems made each order more of a token, rather than an honest preference for Alcos. Time after time, new Alcos had wound up tucked away in some special assignment where they could be watched over more carefully and have less chance of tying up a single track, "hot" main. By 1968, Alco's very survival as a diesel manufacturer was understandably questionable. The C630's, such as 6326 (above) at Gallitzin, 8/68 hadn't performed well, but PRR/PC would give it one more try. (Below) C630 6318 and the conclusion of the PC - Alco alliance; new Century 636 6342 at Weehawken, October 1968.

R. J. Yanosey

155

R. J. Yanosey

C636
6330 - 6344

Pennsy did give Alco still one more chance just before the merger when it ordered yet another 15 of Alco's latest C-C units. Delivered in February through April 1968, the units arrived in Penn Central "colors." The big Alcos matched the SD45's 3600 hp with only 16 cylinders and utilized the advanced "high adhesion" trucks. It was not enough, however, and one year later in 1969, Alco admitted defeat and exited the new locomotive business for all time.

(Above) PC 6338 models a C636 at Secaucus, N.J., May 1976. (Below) The same 6338 departs Bing-hamton, N.Y. coupled to a PC GP35 enroute to Secaucus. All of this was just after Conrail's startup when "power pools" often got mixed up.

T. Trencansky, Herbert H. Harwood Collection

R. J. Yanosey

U25C
6500 - 6519

Pennsy shared almost 1/5 of the relatively small U25C production (20 of the 113 units manufactured). Like the U25B it was based on, the U25C was a pioneering diesel that was subsequently followed by similar models from EMD and Alco. Production started in September 1963 and continued until December 1965. Smooth, clean lines and the familiar early U25 one piece windshield characterize these handsome diesels. PRR's 20 entered PC with the same numbers, as shown at left with class locomotive 6500 at Kearny, N.J., October 1976.

(Below) 2nd U25C 6501 already wears PC black in June 1968 as it and a PRR SD45 get a westbound out of Enola Yard. The first five cars are special company owned flat cars equipped for handling railroad ties.

Herbert H. Harwood

In the photo at left, U25C 6503 and newer Century 636 6342 give a ride to a solid boxcar and reefer train through the familiar PRR landscape at Perdix, Pa. on May 31, 1969. This train is westbound on track 4 of a four track main conspicuously absent of welded rail in 1969.

M. S. Zak Collection

D. T. Walker

J. W. Swanberg

(Center) U25C 6509 and slightly younger sister U28C 6525 enter the yard at Northumberland, Pa. elephant style, on March 23, 1975.

(Right) Work is being performed on U25C 6514 at the Cedar Hill, New Haven, Ct. engine terminal. Five years after the merger (April 7, 1974), the units in the background that can be identified, are all ex NH at this former NH facility.

U25C 6510 was caught working in two different locations during one week in 1970. At right, the massive U boat is laying down a blanket of black exhaust as it starts into a curve heading westbound through Cove, Pa. on September 5, 1970. The big one piece windshield is readily apparent in this photo. In future upgraded GE models, the windshield would be split into two separate pieces to avoid the high cost of replacement when breakage occurred.

(Below) One week earlier the same 6510 (and perhaps the same trailing EMD...units often stayed lashed together for several weeks) enters Frankford Jct., in North Philadelphia, August 30, 1970. The train has come over from the Camden, N.J. Pavonia Yard which PC and PRSL shared, via the Delair Bridge, and will enter the Northeast Corridor at "Shore" Interlocking. This route is known as the Delair Branch.

M. S. Zak Collection

M. S. Zak Collection

U28C
6520 - 6534

R. J. Yanosey

During the year 1966, GE produced its interim U28C model, of which PRR signed up for 15 units. Distinguished from U25C's by a two piece windshield, a new truck and a slight bulge over the radiator, the U28C's were conveyed to PC without number change. Actually, none of PRR's second generation six axle power had to be renumbered under PC since there was no integration from the other two roads.

(Right) U28C 6520, first in the series, sits in the ex RDG Rutherford, Pa. yard in October 1976.

(Center) 6522 leads a mix of GE six axles through East Vandergrift, Pa. 8/74 with the first of four westbound ore trains for the B&LE and the U.S. Steel sintering plant at Saxonburg, Pa. After a shipload of the Venezuelan iron ore was disgorged at the docks in South Philadelphia, it often took three or four trains to transport it west.

(Bottom) Almost 4 years later, in March 1978, the same 6522 is now coupled to three B&M GP9's on a PC-B&M run through at Minoa, N.Y.

R. J. Yanosey

T. Trencansky, Herbert H. Harwood Collection

(Top) The relatively smooth long hood of U28C 6524 contrasts sharply with the "winged" radiator long hood of a new U33C at "AR" Tower, Gallitzin, Pa., August 1968, as the two pushers await either an eastbound freight or a light trip down the mountain.

(Center) TT-1 and TT-2 were the first all piggyback trains in the East. TT-1 has cleared "Benny" interlocking and is approaching the tunnel at the top of the mountain, Tunnelhill, Pa. Power is U28C 6533 still in PRR paint, as is trailing SD40 6053, then surprise Burlington GP30 959 and new PC U33C 6550. Following are 75 piggybacks, NYC caboose 21026 and SD45 pusher 6172. It's 11:09 a.m. October 2, 1968 and if you look closely you can see rear end pushers riding down on PG34 at "Benny."

(Left) Judging by the tire marks in the maintenance road below, March has had its usual mix of rain, snow, and sunshine, as U28C 6534 and a Century 636 enter Enola under the Overview Road bridge, March 20, 1971.

161

M. S. Zak Collection

U30C
6535 - 6539

PRR managed to order five of GE's 1967 3000 hp U30C models. Externally, the U30C is almost identical to the earlier U28C's PRR ordered, so are best identified by their numbers 6535-6539. A FDL-16 powered U30C # 6539 is shown in the photo at left at Camden, N.J., May 27, 1972. The PRR Keystones have been removed, but the Brunswick green and yellow/gold numbers under the cab window remain.

J. Armstrong, Herbert H. Harwood Collection

R. J. Yanosey

(Center) U30C 6538 and an SD45 await dispatching along with ex NYC GP30 2197 on an adjoining freight at DeWitt Yard, Syracuse, N.Y., November 1974.

(Right) The 6536 shakes the wood framed tower building at "Jacks," Mt. Union, Pa. with a westbound as evening sets on a summer day in August 1976. "Jacks" is named after a local 18th century Indian Trader, Captain Jack Armstrong.

In 1968, GE once again raised the horsepower on its models, this time to 3300 hp. Like its B-B brother the U33B, the U33C is also characterized by large "wings" on the long hood above the radiator. Only 2 weeks after the official merger date, the railroad started receiving new U33C's in factory fresh PC black. Ordered by the PRR, the very first U33C built, PC 6540 (left), is enroute for "set up" at Renovo, Pa., February 17, 1968. The Pennsylvania Railroad missed adding yet another diesel type to its history by only a few days.

M. S. Zak Collection

R. J. Yanosey

R. J. Yanosey

(Center) Weathering has caused the first paint job of U33C 6541, now the property of Conrail, to show through in this September 1977 photo at Secaucus, N.J.

(Right) U33C 6560 shown at Weehawken, in October 1968, was the first of a true Penn Central order for U33C's in August 1968.

Back to that top shot again; many fans think PC initially started the merger off with the "red P" scheme and then later simplified it to all white. The 6540 shot demonstrates that this was not the case. All white "P and C" was standard at the beginning, only to be temporarily replaced by a red P or orange C experimental stage in mid 1968. After the colored letter experiments were dropped, PC *resumed* all white.

R. J. Yanosey

No, this is not a Conrail freight. In 1973, Penn Central, anxious to elimi-nate their engine facilities and eventually everything else at Maybrook, N.Y., arranged a run through agreement with the Erie Lackawanna. For many years, the former New Haven and Erie Railroads had interchanged an immense amount of New England traffic at the Maybrook "gateway." PC, desperate for merger economies, was not about to divert traffic to EL that could be run via the former NYC Boston & Albany route to New Eng-land. The Maybrook interchange was supposed to be maintained by ICC mandate as a merger condition, however, and as the traffic shrunk, EL

sought relief. PC consequently came up with this halfway plan which eliminated Maybrook's terminal facilities by establishing a pair of run through trains, NE-97 and NE-74. Until the Poughkeepsie Bridge fire made it a moot question, these trains would pool EL and PC power between Port Jervis, N.Y. (EL) and Cedar Hill, New Haven, Ct. (PC). (Above) NE-97 with U33C's from both roads awaits an EL crew at May-brook yard in April 1973. (Below) The same NE-97 underway on the EL Graham Line at Campbell Hall, N.Y..

R. J. Yanosey

(Left) An eastbound headed by U33C 6549 comes into the interlocking limits of "View" at Duncannon, Pa, May 29, 1971.

(Center, below) One territory on the former NYC that fit the six axle diesel well was the mountainous Boston & Albany. Since the big GE's were based out of Selkirk, N.Y. (outside of Albany), they frequently could be found on the head ends of B&A freights. Here, for example, a U33C-U30C-SD45-U25C combination headed by the 6552 climbs the grade outside Pittsfield, Massachusetts in May 1976. You can actually see the "bow" in the train about 25 cars back.

M. S. Zak Collection

J. Armstrong, Herbert H. Harwood Collection

R. J. Yanosey

U33C 6555, about six months old, matches noses with fellow GE, U30B 2852, a 1967 Erie graduate at Weehawken in October, 1968. Obviously, there is much in common despite the model difference and the paint schemes.

165

Herbert H. Harwood Collection

H24-66
6700 - 6708

In 1956, anxious to find the unit that would give the coup de grace to steam, PRR signed up for 9 Fairbanks Morse Train Masters. The opposed piston giants had many attributes that could reduce the units necessary for this task, but the move to standardization and past experience gave the nod to the EMD GP9 for elimination of steam. The PRR's H24-66's soon found themselves in those "pockets" which kept oddball units out of the system-wide pool of road units. By the time of Penn Central, these FM's still had their original, traditional PRR paint, but had at least traded their 8699-8707 numbers for 6700-6708 in preparation for the merger. The 6700 (above) saw service for Penn Central at 59th Street, Chicago in early 1969, but most met their fate very early on in Penn Central, like 6703, (below), in the East Altoona scrapline, July 1968. 6700, by the way, would go on to outlast all other PC Train Masters, eventually being renumbered 6799 to make room for new U23C's before scrapping in 1970.

William J. Brennan, RJY Collection

U23C
6700 - 6718

By 1970 Penn Central realized that it did no good to run the wheels off a train out on the road and then have it wait hours outside of town for yard space. Penn Central yards, at that time, and continually all through the road's existence, were a place for derailments and delay. The two 1970 orders for 19 2300 hp GE U23C's recognized this and were intended strictly for use as "hump engines" (nevertheless, both the U23C's and SD38's did see occasional, infrequent work as road power in order to clean accumulated carbon deposits out of their engines).

R. J. Yanosey

R. J. Yanosey

Herbert H. Harwood Collection

(Top) The 6705 is an example shown at Enola, July 1973. The GE has a U30 carbody with a 12 rather than 16 cylinder FDL engine.

(Center) U23C's 6715 and 16 drag a freight cut west, prior to shoving them slowly over the Selkirk, N.Y. hump in October, 1973.

(Left) The engineer of U23C 6707 leans out to watch for the hump signal to push his cut of cars back into Enola yard, June 1976.

167

RSD5
6800 - 6805

The half dozen RSD5's that Penn Central inherited from PRR were really only C-C versions of the more popular RS3. The units, built in 1952-53, were chiefly used by Penn Central in the former NYC Buffalo and Syracuse terminals as hump locomotives and heavy switchers. (Above) 1600 hp 6804 awaits some mechanical work outside the enginehouse in Frontier Yard, Buffalo, N.Y., April 1977.

(Below) Two RSD5's, 6802 & 6805, have yarded their transfer and now scurry back through the yard with their hack, at Buffalo, March 1974.

M. S. Zak Collection

Penn Central operated both the DL600A or RSD7 (6806-6810), and the DL600B or RSD15 (6811-6816). Externally, the 2400 hp ex PRR units are identical, and on PC both saw use like other C-C first generation minority makes, as hump, transfer or heavy switching engines. (Above) DL600B 6814 at Selkirk, N.Y. 11/21/71, is the same one pictured behind the PRR SD45 in the color section, page 128.

(Below) A far cry from its original intended use as a passenger train helper in the Alleghenies, PC 6816 was used as a large switcher when photographed at Camden's Pavonia Yard, November 1975. Like the sewer worker resetting the manhole cover with a road stripe on it, some mechanic has created a new PC logo by crisscrossing two hood doors.

DL600
6806 - 6816

R. J. Yanosey

DL702
6855 - 6879

The DL702 or RSD12, as the name implies, is a C-C version of the DL701 or RS11. Pennsy purchased 25 of these ALCOS for Allegheny pusher service and heavy yard/transfer assignments shortly after their 1956 debut. Using only 12 cylinders instead of 16, the DL702 produced only 1800 hp vs the 2400 of the DL600. It did appear to give more satisfactory service however, and the DL702 could often be found in road service, albeit secondary freights, in and around the former PRR eastern terminals.

(Above) DL702 6870 wore a faded "red P" on September 21, 1971 at Camden, N.J. The 6877 (right) is in more customary PC paint in May 1977, Morrisville, Pa. At this point in 6877's career, its very existence depended on not having an expensive mechanical failure. (Below) DL702 6872 and DL701 7637 enter the Northeast Corridor eastbound at Morrisville, May 13, 1970.

The 6875 (right) is adorned by only a nose herald, in this short hood forward view of a westbound freight at Trenton, the State Capitol of NJ, on Columbus Day 1971. Under Penn Central, the DL702's worked principally out of Baltimore, Philadelphia, Camden, and Morrisville, although isolated units could also be found in Selkirk, Syracuse and Buffalo.

(Below) Two Alco 251B engines supply power to 12 axles to move this westbound freight on number three track outside Trenton on January 18, 1976. Compare the track here with the shot on top of page 158, at Perdix, Pa. . . all continuous welded rail here, all government funded.

Both, M.S. Zak Collection

SD9
6900 - 6924

Pennsy picked up 25 of the 1750 hp SD9's for their advertised Special Duty characteristics. Purchased in 1957-58, the units replaced 2-10-0 I1a's in yard and hump service, and seldom saw mainline freight work. Previously numbered in the PRR 7600 series, the SD9's were shifted to 6900-6924 for the merger. The six thousand ID was a handy device to alert crews to the many six axle diesel restrictions on light track and trestles in the Special Instructions of the Timetable.

At right, SD9 6913 at Camden in June of 1975.

Below, SD9's 6809 and 6913 switch their train over to number 2 track prior to entering the ever interesting, Morrisville Yard on February 21, 1971.

R. J. Yanosey

M.S. Zak Collection

SD38
6925 - 6959

Along with the U23C, in 1970 the Penn Central also bought an EMD model for heavy yard and hump service - the 2000 hp, SD38. Thirty five of the 16 cylinder 645 engined SD38's went to such assignments mostly in the western part of the system. Riding on the same frame as the SD40, the SD38 also has that "platform" look at each end. This came in handy in yard service anyway.

(Left) The 6941 at Indianapolis, Ind. July 24, 1971. Naturally, Penn Central prudently saved monies by avoiding dynamic brakes on these yard captive units.

(Below) SD38 6951 sits between crews with another PC yard habitue, a GP9B, this time the 3821 at Elkhart, Ind. July 1970.

RJY Collection

Lee Hastman, Herbert H. Harwood Collection

AS616
6966 - 6976

The 1600 hp AS616 was produced from 1950 to 1954 by the Baldwin-Lima-Hamilton Corporation, located just outside Philadelphia, Pa. Naturally, long time Baldwin loyalist, PRR purchased the unit, of which 1/2 dozen still survived at the time of the PC merger. By that time, however, all Baldwins were suspect and generally were run until an expensive major repair was necessary and sidelined the unit.

(Above) 6974 was the only AS616 to receive a full coat of PC black. After only a few months of service in this dress, however, it sits outside Striegel in Baltimore, May 1972. The writing by the cab reads: "Ship to Striegel Supply & Equip. Co., Bay View Yard, Balt., Md. B&O Delivery, Sales Ord. 2-00-5039." It would not be resold.

(Below) Already at Bay View Yard and in much better health are these two AS616's still painted PRR in February 1969.

The photos at left and center show two excellent views of PC AS616 6966 at Camden, N.J. in the early fall of 1971. 6966 is particularly intriguing since it has apparently changed trucks in the 2 1/2 years since the photo on opposite page, bottom. In that photo it is wearing the customary Commonwealth trucks that most AS616's came with. Rugged and heavy, the Commonwealth rode very rough. Some later PRR AS616's came with the improved tri-mount style truck shown here, but didn't last as long as 6966 which apparently inherited the footwear from an unfortunate younger brother.

M.S. Zak Collection

M.S. Zak Collection

M.S. Zak Collection

SD7
6950 - 6951 (1st)
6998 - 6999 (2nd)

The two SD7's, PRR purchased for the Madison, Indiana hill are a well known story. The specially ballasted 1500 hp EMD's remained at their post during PC tenure and acquired the standard scheme as shown in this photo of 6998 at Frankfort, Indiana April 21, 1975 (right).

175

M.S. Zak Collection

M.S. Zak Collection

RJ Yanosey

GP9
7000 - 7559

All three predecessors to Penn Central purchased the popular GP9. Pennsy bought them by the hundreds in the mid fifties to kill off the last of steam. Although NYC bought a hefty 176 of the 1750 hp unit, interestingly enough, it actually owned more GP7's, 228. New Haven also bought 30 during its late 1950's flirtation with EMD.

(Top, left) Since the PRR's almost 270 GP9's were in the majority, the PC numbering naturally was based around these units, as example, the very nattily attired 7075 at Camden, 9/28/68.

(Center) New Haven's GP9's were dual service units and most remained in the Boston area for possible passenger use. 7292, however, had been overhauled by PC, steam generator removed in the process. Consequently, the former NH unit was renumbered from the passenger 7500 group to this "more freight like", 7292.

(Left) Former NYC GP9's are readily distinguishable from the other two roads, by their lack of dynamic brakes and the jaunty bell some carried over the headlite. PC 7308, Buffalo, N.Y. April 1977.

In most of the territory that the vast Penn Central served, it almost always seemed to be the dominant carrier in town. Indeed, a case could be (and was) made by some cities that the merger left them with no competitive, alternate rail carrier. Such was the domination of the northeast rail scene by Penn Central. So it was ironic to be confronted by a Penn Central branch deep in the coal country of West Virginia; land certainly not controlled by or even associated with PC. Aside from the Virginian Ry., the other local roads did not warmly embrace the former NYC branch when it initially worked its way southeast out of Columbus, Ohio years ago to cast out a small net of coal branches. Although no stranger to West Virginia, (the Weirton Panhandle area) PC did seem strangely out of place in this Pocahontas region, such as GP9 7120 leaving yard limits outside of Charleston, W. Va. in February 1973.

(Below) Another southern invasion occurred at the Western Maryland—N&W railhead at Hagerstown, Maryland. In this photo, taken in June 1968, GP9 7042 and ex NYC F7 1775 have just brought a freight south from Enola on the Cumberland Valley Branch. The Penn Central units wait in the clear at the ex PRR Showo Yard, as an N&W freight behind long nose forward SD35 1564 gets underway south for Roanoke, Va.

R.J. Yanosey

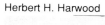

Herbert H. Harwood

(Left) PC 7142 has an odd assortment of characters trailing it through Perdix, Pa., on June 28, 1969. Following the GP9 westward are a GP40, EMD switcher, flat with high/wide load, F7, RS3 and then about 30 bad order freight cars. Apparently a "hospital" train for the Altoona - Hollidsburg area. Naturally, all but GP9 7142 and GP40 3223 are DIT (dead in tow).

At the outset of Conrail and the expected shortages in the locomotive ranks, many PC GP9's were given a reprieve from their secondary duties and saw a return to mainline freight service. One such lucky Geep was 7166, seen (below, center) leading a U33B and U28C west out of Enola in April 1976, Conrail's first month of operation. One month later, the same 7166 locks couplers with GP9 7242 and GP30 2218 at the former CNJ's Elizabethport, N.J. yards. The freight is the CC-7, carrying the traffic off the CNJ's "Chemical Coast" which PC always had covetous eyes on. In fact, well before Conrail, when CNJ was threatening to quit the business, both PC and EL offered to take this portion of the CNJ over. Clearly, that didn't occur.

M.S. Zak Collection

Herbert H. Harwood

R.J. Yanosey

M.S. Zak Collection

(Above) The place and date: Altoona, Pa., May 4, 1969. Penn Central GP9 7161 and GP35 2319 occupy the westbound main separating the yard from the shops prior to tacking on a pusher for the torturous assault on the mountain. It may be 1969, but Altoona still oozes railroading, as spread before you, are car shops, two sets of pushers, a blue flag, position light signals, a westbound coal train, a DIT F7B, and countless other bits of what made railroading so compelling. Unfortunately, the yard tracks with their ties covered with years of accumulated dirt and debris should not be a part of such a scene and signal this would not go on forever. It didn't.

(Below) A single GP9, 7173, is in charge of this Philadelphia Electric high/wide shipment eastbound on the Columbia and Port Deposit Branch along the Susquehanna River, east of Peach Bottom, Pa., July 1976. Billing, carding, routing and handling of over clearance freight cars was a process carefully covered in PC's 207-C Clearance Authority and monitored by the Philadelphia "Clearance Desk."

Herbert H. Harwood

179

Herbert H. Harwood

Ray Hubert, Herbert H. Harwood Collection

(Top) Class engine, ex Pennsy 7000, re-
laxes between assignments with a PRR
"cabin" at Orrville, Ohio, July 1970.

(Center) In 1971, ex NH GP9 7555 awaits
the Monday morning rush in the engine
terminal at Hartford, Ct. By the way, that
"interim" black hood, red cab PC scheme,
was one of the nicest.

(Right) PC 7327, the ex NYC 5927, brings
a PRR hopper northward on the Mahoning
Secondary Track and crosses the ex PRR
(PFt. W&C) mainline to Chicago, at Alliance, Ohio in June 1971.

D. Hamley, Herbert H. Harwood Collection

R.J. Yanosey

Edward Hunt, Herbert H. Harwood Collection

For the 1974 and '75 football seasons, Penn Central and the Massachusetts Bay Transportation Authority teamed up to haul Boston football lovers out to Foxboro, Ma., home of the New England Patriots (Schaefer Stadium). This eight car special shown at Mansfield, Ma. on September 28, 1975 is drawn by three ex NH GP9's led by the 7530.

M.S. Zak Collection

DL701
7600 - 7674

R.J. Yanosey

R.J. Yanosey

For a diesel of which only 327 were built total, it is interesting to note that all three Penn Central predecessors managed to purchase the DL701 or RS11. In early 1956, Alco released its new 1800 hp DL701 in obvious one-ups-manship to the sales dominating 1750 hp EMD GP9. The handwriting was on the wall for Alco, however, as PRR purchased 270 GP9's but only 38 DL701's; NYC's score was even worse 176 to 9 in favor of the Geep; New Haven, 30 GP9's to 15 DL701's.

(Top) Class locomotive 7600 is an ex NYC unit at Selkirk, N.Y. November 21, 1971. NYC was so disgusted with these new Alcos that they cancelled the order mid through, compelling Alco to sell the remainder to the Delaware & Hudson Ry.

(Center) PC 7639 is an ex PRR specimen sitting in a deadline of Alcos one month before Conrail, March 1976 at Kearny, N.J.

(Bottom) DL701 7667 displays the distinctive NH Hancock air whistle above the engineers window at Maybrook, N.Y. in April 1973. Note that all three units are on the rails of their former owners at different times during Penn Central, and that while NH thought the short hood end the "F" end, NYC and PRR used the long hood.

The Belvidere Delaware Branch of the Penn Central was an extremely scenic line running through an abundance of early Americana. Leaving the ex PRR NE Corridor at "Fair" in Trenton, N.J. the Bel-Del, as it was more commonly known, made its way north about 10 miles until reaching the point where our first president made his journey across the Delaware River, aptly named, Washington's Crossing, N.J. Further north, it passed through Lambertville an antique center and junction with the Black River & Western RR, and then past the gentlemans' farms at Stockton, N.J.

Always paralleling the Delaware & Raritan Canal, a northbound train, such as Extra 7627 (above) reaches Raven Rock, where the Delaware River was dammed in the early 19th century to give the canal an endless source of water.

(Below) PC DL701 7627 and big brother DL702 6875 pass one of the pleasant all stone stations on the Bel-Del, this one at Milford, N.J. on May 2, 1971. After a few miles further north, the Bel-Del comes into Phillipsburg, N.J. and a connection with the several lines that ran there: LV, CNJ and L&HR.

Most of the DL701's seldom ventured into scenery such as the Bel-Del offered, instead performing rugged transfer service throughout urban terminals in the northeast day in and day out. The photos on this page illustrate such work:

3600 hp, generated by two DL701's, gets a transfer rolling, made up chiefly of gondolas from Bethlehem Steel's Sparrows Point plant. This is Baltimore, November 1972. Observe that in this and the center photo, the units are set up in standard PRR practice so the "F" end will always lead regardless of the direction the lash up heads in.

Herbert H. Harwood, RJY Collection

A DL701-GP9B-DL701 combination headed by ex PRR 7634 gets underway with a coal train at Baltimore, September 1973.

(Below) PC 7651 leads a Meadows to Waverly transfer, west across the Passaic & Harsimus Branch, Newark, N.J., in September 1976.

Herbert H. Harwood, RJY Collection

R.J. Yanosey

R. J. Yanosey

GP38
7675 - 7939

Along with the GP40, SD45 and other more popular units that EMD introduced in 1966 with its 645 engine, there was a unit that did not attract much attention (or buyers). That unit was the 2000 hp non-turbocharged V16, GP38. Along with most other roads, PC ignored the GP38 for several years until a nationwide swing toward fuel and maintenance savings made it a giant seller. PC ordered 240 of the units in the years 1969 to 1971. Cheap to run, and able to see use anywhere on the system, the GP38 became Penn Central's ideal locomotive.

(Top) PC 7800, at Altoona August 1976, typified most PC GP38's; pretty much a stock dynamic brake equipped unit.

R. J. Yanosey

A handful of the GP38's were purchased for more specialized service such as 7906, at Mingo Jct., October 1976, (center) which lacked dynamic brakes, and had a built out front windshield to permit walking space around the control stand in such dual control equipped units.

(Below) One of the first PC GP38's, the 7715, is shown brand new, just south of Cincinnati in Covington, Kentucky. The GP38 has hold of a transfer on the Chesapeake & Ohio mainline at "KC" tower where the L&N comes in. "KC" stands for Kentucky Central, an old L&N subsidiary.

R. J. Yanosey

R.J. Yanosey

(OPPOSITE PAGE) GP38 7756 assisted by a GP9 and a DL701 brings westbound traffic past Anacostia Tower, Washington, D.C. in March 1971. Anacostia tower is on the ex PRR Landover, Md. to South End (RF &P) freight line around the east side of Washington. The tower is at the Anacostia River and controls the junction with the B&O freight line. Anacostia is more famous as the location of the Veteran's encampment that was broken up by General Douglas MacArthur in the early days of the depression. (Herbert H. Harwood)

(THIS PAGE - Above) GP38 7765 leads a PC SD35, a RDG C424, and a PC EMD past "Homer" control point in East Altoona, Pa., August 1976. "Homer" was remotely controlled from "Alto" tower and consisted of switches to the Rose Connecting Track which ran into the yard. Note the presence of EL units in the former PC scrapline during these early Conrail days.

(Below) GP38 7772 leads 4 other GP38's and a C425 down onto the Bessemer & Lake Erie Railroad at East Butler, Pa. in May 1975. The train is one of the thousands of South American iron ore that came over the PC to the U.S. Steel plant at Saxonburg, Pa. for sintering. With that process complete it was ready for use in the nearby steel mills of Pittsburgh.

R.J. Yanosey

(Left) GP38 7774 hurries west at West Leechburg, Pa. in May 1975 with the day's work from the mills and foundries located along the Conernaugh Division. PC gondolas like the ones in this local took a terrific beating at the hands of the crane operators in these mills. After loading a gon full of scrap, SOP called for attaching a concrete block weighing several tons, and dropping this atop the load until it "fit" the gondola. This, of course, did wonders for the car's sides and underframes. It was a hard process for PC to try to stop, and the road was forced to "look the other way," straightening the bulging sides at Hollidaysburg when such a car came in for shopping.

(Below) A little less than a year after this photo was taken (May 1975, at Kiski Jct., Freeport, Pa.) the 7776 became the "Bi-Centennial" locomotive for Conrail. The unit was painted a smart, red, white and blue scheme in May 1976 and escaped most photographers due to the relatively remote assignment of 7776 and the fact it was repainted full Conrail blue by October of that year. With several thousand locomotives in a dozen different paint schemes, Conrail shops were told to repaint anything due for shopping that was not in full blue, and no one thought to make 7776 an exception.

R.J. Yanosey

R.J. Yanosey

GP38 7775 pulls a hopper off a side track at Blairsville, Pa. on a hazy summer morning in August 1976. Although the switch is set against the Geep's movement, it need not be thrown since it is the type which can be thrown over by the wheels of an oncoming movement trailing through it. The crumbling station platform has seen better days, but the station seems to be in use as a base for the track people who use the high rail truck and camp cars in the background.

GP38 7795 leads three GP35's and a PP&L (Penna. Power & Light) unit train eastbound at Allegrippus, just below Gallitzin, Pa. in July 1973. PP&L trains were frequently seen with some low numbered U25C's which were modified with a special "creeper control" for low speed loading of coal at Tunnelton, Pa. on the Conemaugh Division. They also often carried specially painted brown PC cabooses.

In the home of Kellogg's Corn Flakes, PC GP38 7818 singly takes a westbound through the passenger station at Battle Creek, Michigan in September 1972. 7818 was destined to spend 9 years with Conrail, and then in March 1985 it was sold along with 16 other ex PC GP38's to the Pittsburgh & Lake Erie RR.

R.J. Yanosey

Sometimes chasing a freight through the Juniata Valley of central Pennsylvania was an easy task. Due to plenty of out of service tracks while Conrail maintenance people took advantage of their first summer, this eastbound coal train was crossed over at every interlocking or "stabbed" for more important trains.

(Above) PC GP38 7825 assisted by CR'd U25B 2640 crosses her string of Cambria & Indiana hoppers from track 3 to 2 at Mifflin, Pa., August 1976.

(Below) A few short miles east on Route 22, and the same freight is caught again canting through an "S" curve under the Route 333 bridge at Thompsontown, Pa..

R.J. Yanosey

Once again the 7825-2640 coal train, this time at Lewistown, Pa. in August 1976. Lewistown has a very special niche in the history of the Pennsylvania Railroad, for it was here on Saturday, September 1, 1849 that the first PRR passenger train completed its sixty mile journey west from Harrisburg. The train was composed of the Baldwin built "Mifflin" and three wooden passenger cars. For a short time, Lewistown became the western terminus of the new road. Today, this 1849 former freight station at Lewistown stores the archives of the Pennsylvania Railroad Technical & Historical Society, Inc.

R.J. Yanosey

R.J. Yanosey

In many Pennsylvania towns, a visitor can often receive a clue to the town's age by its name. Pittsburgh is a good example. It was founded in 1758 and named after the pre Revolutionary War British statesman, William Pitt. In our center photo, 4 EMD's led by GP38 7835, step smartly through the city named for the Revolutionary War hero Nathanael Greene; Greensburg, Pa. in October 1975. Greensburg generated plenty of traffic for Penn Central, both in town and on the Southwest Secondary, which joined the ex PRR main here.

R.J. Yanosey

(Right) In May 1975, the imposing structure of "Hunt" tower stands guard over the movement of eastbound coal through Huntingdon, Pa. in May 1975. Power is provided by GP38 7839 and an elder GP35.

Robert Malinoski

GP38-2
7940 - 8162

In the beginning of 1972, General Motors began production of its "Dash 2" line of locomotives. While the GP38-2 was internally different from the GP38, externally the only noticeable differences were high adhesion trucks with dampening struts on diagonally opposite trucks, and a "sight glass" located on the long hood, right rear. Penn Central, obviously entralled with the GP38, ordered this improved version, and starting at number 7940 in May 1972, added 223 GP38-2's by October of 1973.

(Above, left) Combined train NE-4/WU-2 is the center of attraction in a busy scene. The units have just passed the site of the old "FY" tower and are on the wooden drawbridge over Overpeck Creek, headed north on the ex NYC West Shore, now called the "River Line" by PC. Public Service Electric & Gas' Ridgefield, N.J. generating station dominates the background, but also visible are the Empire State Building and the World Trade Center over in New York City. To the right, the tracks of the NYS&W (Susquehanna) parallel the River Line. NE-4/WU-2 consists of GP38-2 7942, GP35 2327, GP40 3013 and 109 cars, at 5:50 p.m. Wednesday, May 28, 1975.

(Center, left) Eastbound, past the World Headquarters of a company that contributed enormously to the traffic of Penn Central, comes a GP38-2–NW2 light movement at Woodward Avenue, Detroit, MI. in June 1973.

Elmer Treloar, Herbert H. Harwood Collection

R.J. Yanosey

(Left) Eastbound PE-10 is powered by PC GP38-2 8087 and an ex CNJ SD35 on a rainy day in October, 1976 through the borough of East Vandergrift, Pa. The Conemaugh Division tracks, on which PE-10 rides, is the only PC mainline guarded solely by cab signals, as relayed by the signal case at left. The entire division was devoid of wayside signals except at interlockings.

(At right) PP&L hoppers are returning to a mine on the Cresson Secondary and are led by PC GP38-2 8100, a CR'd GP40 3011, PC GP38-2's 8042 and 8148, and GP35 2277, Cresson, Pa., August 1976. Note the two different whistle signs signifying the impending crossing at grade and the requirements of Rule 14; — —— 0 ——.

In addition, we call your attention to that second unit, GP40 3011. This ubiquitous diesel has popped up in 4 photos, taken by 4 different photographers in 3 different paint schemes, (pages 58, 154 and here). And as a final salute, this "good runner" showed up in a lashup in the midst of the dispatcher sheet tally (UFY 623/96PP&L hoppers) on page 246. It happens to all fans at one time or another (a particular diesel showing up seemingly everywhere).

R.J. Yanosey

D.T. Walker

Herbert H. Harwood

(Center, above) GP38-2 8107 leads an eastbound TOFC train through West Brookfield, Mass. on the onetime Boston & Albany main line. The large frame building behind is the original 1839 station, built by the Western Railroad of Massachusetts. Replaced by a stone station in the 1890's and later slightly altered, it may be the oldest surviving passenger station in the United States (B&O's 1831 Ellicott City, Md. station, though older, originally was a freight station).

(Left) About one month into Conrail, April 29, 1976 to be exact, GP38-2 8133 comes down the "Ought" track as it returns to its train, visible on number two track of the NEC, after leaving off a few cars at the Ford Yard in Metuchen, N.J. The overhead structure carries the aptly named "Bridge Street."

Herbert H. Harwood

(Above) In October 1974, a westbound coal train with a GP38-2, DL701, GP30, GP9B, GP30 combo, crosses the Gunpowder River Trestle, near Edgewood, Md. In a few hundred yards the 8156 will be at the future site of the January 4, 1987 wreck of Amtrak #94, "The Colonial," which cost the lives of 16 passengers. Caused by the eastbound "Colonial" slamming into three Conrail freight diesels at an estimated 128 mph, the accident would have certainly been much worse if it had occurred out here on the bridge.

(Below) Bill Moore, PC's new President after the bankruptcy, hailed from the Southern Ry, where second generation diesels were customarily run long hood forward; so consequently, some GP38-2's purchased during his tenure on Penn Central, were equipped with dual controls and set up to operate in that manner. Emerging from the North Avenue B&P Tunnel, Baltimore in August 1976, GP38-2 8160, part of that order, leads an empty hopper train eastward. The hoppers came from electric power plants in southern Maryland on the Pope's Creek Branch and are now enroute back to the coal mines of Pennsylvania

Herbert H. Harwood

194

8000 Series: Baldwin and Small EMD Switchers

For our purposes of carrying this book forward in numerical sequence, the high 7000, low 8000 series becomes a small area of exceptions. This is caused by the fact that Penn Central had numbered its Baldwins in the high 7000's (in the 1966 plan), not anticipating both the longevity of the rugged Eddystone products, and the ever increasing numbers of GP38's and 38-2's which started at number 7675 (well below the first Baldwin at 7800). The invading GP38 army caused PC to continually renumber upwards its remaining fleet of Baldwins, causing some to eventually see three renumberings under PC before their demise. For this book, with 20/20 hindsight available, we have separated the GP38/GP38-2's from the Baldwins.

DS44-660

7800 - 7885 (1st)
8350 - 8380 (2nd)

While both NYC and PRR had purchased the products of Baldwin and successor Baldwin-Lima-Hamilton, Pennsy took claim to the dubious title of the biggest Baldwin owner of all major railroads. This status was obvious in the cast of PC's Baldwin fleet. At the top, right, PC 8351 at Camden, October 17, 1970 was an ex PRR Baldwin DS44-660. The DS44-660 was built 1946-49 in Baldwin's standard postwar carbody. The "DS" designation died with Baldwin Locomotive Works, and after 1951 Baldwin-Lima-Hamilton simply used an "S" prefix with the first two numbers of the horsepower.

DS44-750

7886 - 7913 (1st)
8381 - 8388 (2nd)

(Center) DS44-750 stood for Diesel Switcher, two trucks of 4 wheels each, 750 horsepower. It was manufactured by Baldwin from 1949-51. PC 7887 was an example of this ex PRR model, photographed in Philadelphia in 1969.

(Right) PC 8381 illustrates the ultimate fate of most Baldwins during the Penn Central seventies. Orphaned and out of place in an all GM, GE world, the Baldwins were written off the roster at the first expensive mechanical failure. 8381, an ex PRR DS44-750, has survived Penn Central barely intact, but will see no service for Conrail. Sitting in weeds minus her trucks, the unit serves as a parts supply for the two Baldwin switches of the Warner Sand Company, outside Morrisville, Pa. May 1976.

M.S. Zak Collection

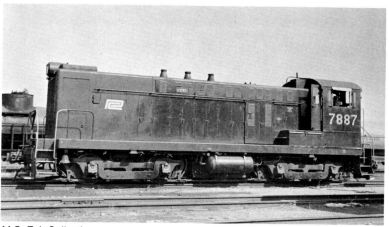

M.S. Zak Collection

R.J. Yanosey

S12

8094 - 8199 (1st)
8307 - 8344 (2nd)

In 1951, BLH introduced a turbocharged 1200 hp switcher designated S12 which was purchased by both PRR and NYC.

(Top, right) PC 8096 was a former NYC S12 shown at New Castle, Pa., August 30, 1969. From 1947 till the end of production Baldwin adopted a standard carbody which made the various DS44-1000 and S12 units virtually identical externally.

(Center) PC 8193 shown at Baltimore, July 1971 was the former PRR 8743, a flat front S12.

(Below) In September 1968, three S12's still in traditional PRR dress handle a transfer at Bay View Yard, Baltimore.

M.S. Zak Collection

Herbert H. Harwood, RJY Collection

Herbert H. Harwood, RJY Collection

In this photo, S12 8117, the former PRR 8977, wears a fresh coat of 13D PC black at Wilmington, Del. January 12, 1969.

M.S. Zak Collection

William J. Brennan, RJY Collection

(Center) The S12 was virtually identical in external appearance with the earlier DS44-1000. By July 1974, this DS44-1000 had seen several waves of GP38/38-2's arrive. Numbered 8274 in this Camden, N.J. photo, the unit was formerly PC 7996.

(Left) Both the S12 and DS44-1000 had the standard Baldwin postwar carbody which encompassed a flat front end with front radiator. Both also shared a distinctive feature: a big turbocharger stack set off to the left side of the unit. The 8277, eastbound at Camden August 19, 1972, wears a band of new black under the window number due to the fact that the DS44-1000 was recently renumbered from 8007 to make room for a GP38-2.

(Left) PC 8339, a BLH S12, sits in a dead-line at Camden, October 1975 with a crane poised ominously in the back-ground. By 1975, Camden was the sole refuge of Baldwin power. With a nearby BLH parts supply and a mechanical staff well versed in De La Vergne engines, Camden kept Baldwin's name on PC's roster until Conrail arrived in 1976.

R.J. Yanosey

DS44-1000

7916 - 8046 (1st)
8263 - 8297 (2nd)

The DS44-1000 was manufactured 1946-51 by Baldwin Locomotive Works in both 8 and 6 cylinder versions.

M.S. Zak Collection

Herbert H. Harwood, RJY Collection

In the center photo above, PC 7955 was a 1000 hp, model DS44-1000 photo-graphed at Wilmington, De., February 28, 1970.

(Left) PC 8037 was also an ex PRR DS44-1000 shown in a balder scheme at Baltimore, March 1972.

M.S. Zak Collection

LIMA/EMD
8062 - 8063 (1st)
8398 - 8399 (2nd)

In 1950, the railroads still had not learned the value of standardization, and the worthiness of some diesel manufacturers. A longtime, outstanding builder of steam locomotives, the Lima Locomotive Works of Lima, Ohio made a quick about face in 1949 and merged with the Hamilton Corporation, a manufacturer of diesel engines. NYC purchased 16 of their light road switchers, before Lima Hamilton became the LH in Baldwin-Lima-Hamilton in 1951. By 1957, NYC was much more sophisticated in the world of diesels and attempted to rebuild two of the LH Roadswitchers with

EMD 567C engines while retaining their 1200 hp rating. The repowering was successful in that these two outlasted their 14 pure LH brethren, surviving on into Penn Central. Apparently, PC thought it successful also, as the two units saw much the same service as straight EMD switchers, even taking a stint as passenger car switchers at busy 30th Street, Philadelphia. (Above) The 8062 sits at Camden on September 12, 1971. (Below) Sister 8063, also at Camden, 9/25/71.

M.S. Zak Collection

M.S. Zak Collection

(Above) PC 8062, one of two examples of a 1200 hp Lima Hamilton Light Road Switcher rebuilt with a EMD engine, brings a westbound string of gondolas into the yard at Morrisville, Pa. on September 20, 1969. Gondolas frequented Morrisville which was adjacent to the colossal U.S. Steel Fairless Works.

(Below) The two Lima/EMD's 8062-8063 were caught up in the same renumbering problem occasioned by the GP38/38-2 arrivals. By August 26, 1973 when this photo was taken in South Philadelphia, the 8000 series GP38-2's were on the property and the 8063 had been renumbered 8399.

M.S. Zak Collection

DRS44-1000

8050 - 8053 (1st)
8300 - 8302 (2nd)

The two Baldwin light road switchers, the BLW DRS44-1000 and the BLH RS12 are indistinguishable and both were rostered by Penn Central. Although both PRR and NYC purchased the RS12, only PRR rostered the rare DRS44-1000 (6 of 9 total produced). PC 8053 (top, right) shown at Camden May 27, 1972 is an example of this rare model purchased only by PRR, TC and CP.

(Right) PC 8302, a DRS44-1000, was PC 8052 before the GP38 caused renumbering. Photographed at Wilmington, De., September 1975.

M.S. Zak Collection

Herbert H. Harwood, RJY Collection

Herbert H. Harwood, RJY Collection

RS12

8067 - 8091 (1st)
8303 - 8306 (2nd)

The 8082, pictured left , is a more common RS12, formerly owned by the New York Central as their 6235. It is shown at Baltimore in October 1972. Interestingly, NYC had repowered some 1500 hp Baldwin Roadswitchers with EMD prime movers in the mid fifties. In contrast to the Lima/EMD experience, these never reached Penn Central ownership, but some lighter, "pure" RS12 Baldwins did.

201

Herbert H. Harwood

As the '70's got underway, Penn Central concentrated the shrinking Baldwin fleet in the Camden-Philadelphia terminal area, as well as Wilmington and Baltimore. Baltimore provided some good "Baldwin watching" opportunities. (Above) PC RS12 8305, the former PC 8082 and NYC 6235, switches a bulk head flat car at Bay View yard within Baltimore in November 1972. By 1972 the 8300 series numbers once worn by PC H12-44's was now available for these displaced Baldwins.

(Below) RS12 8304, sporting new black paint over the former number PC 8073, has a hold of Clearance Car 28205 at Baltimore Station in February 1973. The many tight tunnels in the City of Baltimore were always a source of problems, mainly leaks requiring masonry work, and hence constant clearance checks. Baltimore's majestic marble station was opened in September 1911 as a part of A. J. Cassatt's extensive improvements of the Washington- New York City route during that time.

Herbert H. Harwood

H10-44
8207-8260

Both NYC and PRR contributed handfuls of H10-44 switchers to the Penn Central cause in 1968. This handsome smooth lined 1000 hp switcher was styled by the great Raymond Loewy (of GG1 fame), and manufactured after WWII until 1949. Used 1968-1971 by Penn Central, apparently only one ex NYC FM switcher, H12-44 8315, saw a PC paint job, as the rest were scrapped by 1971 in their former owner's dress.

(Top, right)   The 8244 is an H10-44, the former PRR 9080, and is shown at Chicago, April 12, 1968.

(Center)   H10-44 8248 has found the Chicago nesting grounds for FM's and rests at 59th Street in March 1968 in the company of a DM&IR SD9 leased by PC during these early, power-short days after the merger.

(Below) Exactly one year later H10-44 8259 shares the engine terminal at Hammond, Ind. with some units painted PC. Obviously, someone had made a decision to exclude 8259 from that club.

RJY Collection

M.S. Zak Collection

RJY Collection

H12-44 8301 (left) missed the PC roster by just a few days. It was photographed in very early 1968 at GE's Erie, Pa. deadline.

RJY Collection

M.S. Zak Collection

RJY Collection

The H12-44 was a two hundred horsepower improvement over the H10 introduced by Fairbanks Morse in 1950. The photos on this page are excellent examples of the roof overhang so characteristic of the early FM switchers. Although normally thought of as an H10-44 attribute, the first 2 1/2 years of H12-44 production also had this feature. (Above, center) H12-44 8312 awaits the torch in the scrapline at E. Altoona June 18, 1969.

(Left) H12-44 8323 rests at 59th Street Chicago, on April 12, 1969. The unit it is coupled to, appears to have been used for parts picking to keep the others running. Although the carbody, underframe and trucks might be scrapped, more likely the opposed piston engine found use somewhere, as they were greatly in demand on the used marine engine market. FM diesel locomotives would sometimes be seen enroute DIT to distant points as it was often easier to use the unit as a bed to transport the desired OP engine, and scrap the remains after arrival. LIRR's C-Liners were seen in western Pennsylvania in 1963 enroute to Texas in just such a move.

RJY Collection

Chicago was certainly the place to catch Penn Central FM's in the late sixties. It was the proverbial "elephant's burial ground." All FM models that PC stabled soon found their way to the Windy City where they served until the last one died in 1971.

(Above) H12-44's of two different styles and owners lock knuckles at the 59th Street Terminal on April 12, 1969. While the NYC 8307 looks well preserved, the PRR 8342's days appear numbered. The 8342 was one of the later H12-44's purchased by Pennsy (2/54) and lacks the curved fairing over the battery box.

(Below) The 8327 was a November '52 H12-44 and although it lacks the overhanging roof and has a squarer look than the NYC H12-44's, on the opposite page, it still retains the curved battery box fairing. Shown at Chicago 2/24/68.

M.S. Zak Collection

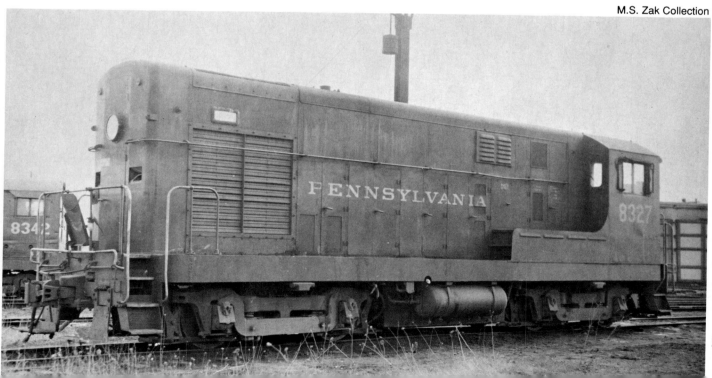

R.J. Yanosey

The little 600 hp SW1 was a popular unit with both the NYC and PRR. This early successful switcher was characterized by a sandbox which protruded out under the front grillwork.

Penn Central had the ex NYC SW1's in the 8400 series (8400-8500) like 8461 (top) at Camden 11/75 and the ex PRR units in the 8500 series (8501-8599) such as 8558 (center) at Enola 3/28/70.

(Below) PC SW1 8413 has a small switch run in hand at South Station, Boston in July 1974.

M. S. Zak Collection

Herbert H. Harwood

(Right) SW1 8487 rests in Saginaw, Michigan August 21, 1971 in the company of one of those little cabooses specially made by PC for yard and transfer duties.

(Center) SW1 8519 models a unique paint scheme at Newberry Jct., Pa., April 23, 1969. Such disparate paint schemes were not officially sanctioned but resulted from creative repaintings done in small shops where the proper stencils or decals were lacking.

(Bottom) SW1 8559 switches the carfloat at Little Creek, Va. in November, 1972. The ex PRR float yard at Little Creek (just outside Norfolk, Va., several miles north of the Chesapeake Bay Bridge Tunnel) was located right in the middle of a Navy Amphibious Base. A small PC switcher like 8559 would offload the cars which had been floated over across Chesapeake Bay from PC's line down the Delmarva Penninsula, and the Norfolk-Portsmouth Belt Line would make connections with other local lines in Norfolk. Note the incoming jet, making this one of those all transport mode shots . . .train, ship, airplane.

RJY Collection

M.S. Zak Collection

H.W. Serig, Herbert H. Harwood Collection

SW8
8600-8627

After the little SW1, the EMD switcher assumed a look-alike carbody which several successive models carried during the 1940's and 50's. Produced in enormous quantities, this ubiquitous EMD switcher profile was eventually found on all three parent roads. The SW8, which used this carbody however, was purchased only by predecessor NYC. PC 8613 (below), wears the remnant of her NYC paint at Saginaw, MI, November 16, 1971. 8613 was a 800 hp SW8, manufactured in February 1953, powered by a 567B engine.

RJY Collection

MS Zak Collection

SW900
8628-8646

Another EMD, the SW900 was introduced in January 1954 and manufactured until November 1965 with a 8 cylinder 567C engine.

(Left)   8634 is an ex NYC SW900, photographed here awaiting repainting at Collinwood, March 1969. The paper taped on the cab side reads: "Detroit." This was the maintenance base for 8634, but major overhauls like this were performed at Collinwood or Altoona.

M.S. Zak Collection

M.S. Zak Collection

The 1000 hp NW2 was a truly significant diesel manufactured during the ten years from 1939-1949 (although not during WWII). Both PRR and NYC enjoyed the NW2, the first EMD switcher to adopt the more or less standardized carbody, although NW2's differ slightly with their front, half-length radiator grill.

(Top, left) PC 8656 was an ex PRR NW2 photographed at South Philadelphia 3/28/70. All the ex PRR NW2's were numbered in the 8600's; the ex NYC's in the high 8600's, the 87 and 8800's.

(Center) PC 8674, an NW2 manufactured in the fall of 1948, once carried the lettering and number, PRR 9174. Shown at Newberry Jct., Pa. 10/10/76.

(Bottom) PC 8693 is an NW2 with quite a history. Photographed at Rensselaer, N.Y. 12/75 and manufactured in the summer of 1948, the unit spent almost the first ten years of life as New York Ontario & Western 125. When that road folded in 1957, the little EMD was sold to NYC and spent another 10 years as NYC 9510, before being renumbered 8693 prior to the merger.

J. Armstrong, Herbert H. Harwood Collection

Elmer Treloar, Herbert H. Harwood Collection

R.J. Yanosey

(Above) NW2 8767, a late 1948 graduate of LaGrange, trundles past the GM Headquarters at Woodward Avenue, Detroit in June 1973 with a PC yard caboose. Although the EMD is fitting for this photo, locomotive production hardly occupied much time in that building which was mostly devoted to automobiles.

(Center) PC 8799 spent the major portion of her life as an Indiana Harbor Belt locomotive. Almost two years into Conrail (March 1978) the boomer was photographed in full PC paint while on ex CNJ trackage at Elizabethport, N.J.

(Bottom) PC 8806 was also photographed on ex CNJ trackage, this time at Brill's Yard Newark, N.J. in July 1976. 8806 was manufactured at the very end of NW2 production (11/49) and delivered to New York Central.

R.J. Yanosey

(OPPOSITE PAGE) PC 8762 still wears most of her NYC attire as she leads some cars past the Michigan Central Station in Detroit, October 1971 (Elmer Treloar, Herbert H. Harwood Collection).

210

9000 Series: EMD & Alco Switchers

M.S. Zak Collection

M.S. Zak Collection

M.S. Zak Collection

SW7
8836-9098

In late 1949, EMD had announced a successor to the 1000 hp NW2, the 1200 hp SW7. Produced for only a short time (10/49-1/51) the SW7 came at a time when both PRR and NYC were busily replacing steam, and was eagerly purchased by both roads. Penn Central inherited the SW7's from these roads and proceeded to number them spanning both the 8 and 9000 series.

(Above) PC 8837 in full Penn Central garb was a very early SW7 manufactured in January 1950 and purchased by NYC. It is shown here at Bristol, Pa. on February 24, 1974.

(Center, left) SW7 8865 was the property of subsidiary IHB before coming over to parent NYC and then PC. The EMD is one of several known examples of diesels which received a white frame stripe as part of a full Penn Central repainting. It models its different garb in this Chicago 4/10/71 photo.

(Bottom, left) Ex NYC 8883 also had the white frame stripe treatment. Shown April 1969, location unknown.

Two "red P" ex Pennsy SW7's mirror the brief history of the Penn Central in the photos on this page.

(Above) 9080 idles in the yard at Altoona, Pa. in June 1969. Although the merger has been consumated for over a year, and steam has been dead for about a dozen years, there are still PRR tenders around to remind the SW7 of its heritage, and that railroading really hasn't changed that much since steam departed.

(Below) Still adorned with a fading "red P" ex PRR SW7 9077 is photographed at Pitcairn, Pa. in October 1975. "Red P's" which lasted into the seventies tended to fade rather badly into various shades of pink. With less than 5 months to go till "C" day, the unit was undoubtedly one of the very few to reach Conrail bearing this experiment from the early days of the merger.

R.J. Yanosey

M.S. Zak Collection

M.S. Zak Collection

The SW9 was the successor to the SW7 in the EMD catalog from February 1951 till December 1953. Using the 567B engine instead of the SW7's 567A, the SW9 produced 1200 hp and was purchased by both PRR and Central.

(Top) SW9 8941 was the NYC unit of the same number. It was manufactured in February 1952 and shown here at Camden 10/16/76.

(2nd from top) 8962 was also a NYC unit and shows the other side of a SW9 at Camden 4/18/76.

(3rd from top) 8968, an ex NYC SW9 of the same number, is shown at Cleveland, April 1973.

(Bottom) PC 9042 is an ex PRR SW9 shown here at Enola 7/1/73.

T.N. Colbert, Herbert H. Harwood Collection

M.S. Zak Collection

PC SW9 9044 was the ex PRR 8544 before the PC renumbering. The SW9 is shown deep in Pennsylvania Dutch Country, Lancaster, Pa. September 2, 1973. Actually, the Amish and Mennonite residents of Lancaster are not Dutch, but "Deutsch" (German).

M.S. Zak Collection

PC 9061 is also ex PRR and shown at Morrisville, Pa. February 1975.

M.S. Zak Collection

9114 is the ex PRR 8514 in fairly fresh paint at Collinwood 3/15/69. This SW9, assigned to Stanley Yard, outside Toledo, is fitted with a special winterization hatch over the cab window to allow the engineer to get a better view down the train without opening the window during icy winter blasts.

M.S. Zak Collection

Oddly enough, ex PRR SW9 9117 wears a "red P" interim scheme at Collinwood 4/27/70, showing that this logo was not reserved only for full repaints.

M.S. Zak Collection

M.S. Zak Collection

M.S. Zak Collection

In 1969, Penn Central instituted a program to upgrade some 20 year old NW2's to 1200 hp. The veteran EMD's had larger fuel tanks, twin sealed beam headlights, and roller bearings installed and were given the capability to MU with other units. Readily identifiable from the pure NW2's which lacked these features, the rejuvenated EMD's gained a new lease on life and were renumbered mostly into the 9100 series.

PC 9101 shown (left) at Elmira, N.Y. 10/15/71 illustrates the fact that the rebuilds were not always given a full repainting after leaving the shop.

(Below) NW2u 9164 switches Enola Yard on June 28, 1969. Before the upgrading, this unit was PC 8820, a former IHB NW2.

SW1200
9009 - 9199

R.J. Yanosey

Manufactured from January 1954 until 12 years later (May 1966), the SW1200 had a long and successful record. Undoubtedly its sales would have been greater had not steam been almost completely vanquished from the switcher ranks by 1954. Nevertheless, both PRR and NH managed to purchase the unit.

(Top, right) PC 9023 was more or less a stock SW1200 manufactured for PRR in late 1957. Shown here at Altoona in August 1976.

(Center, right) Although the SW1200 was the last of several EMD switcher models purchased by PRR, it was the first (and only) EMD switcher purchased by New Haven. PC SW1200 9186 shown here at West Springfield, Ma. in April 1974 was the ex New Haven 646, a February 1956 EMD product.

(Below) PC 9182 illustrates an ex NH SW1200 in interim paint. The unit is pictured switching former New Haven passenger cars at the station in New Haven, Ct., in February 1971. While it is certainly easy to confuse PRR's standard SW1200's with other similar carbodied EMD's, New Haven's were unmistakable since they rode on those unique Flexicoil road trucks that NH opted for in 1956. The Flexicoils permitted these SW1200's to operate at speeds up to 65 mph. The versatile EMD's were sometimes even used in road service by NH.

J. Armstrong, Herbert H. Harwood Collection

Ray Hubert, Herbert H. Harwood Collection

M.S. Zak Collection

SW1500

9216 - 9227
9500 - 9583

In 1966, in conjunction with its introduction of its 645 engine line, EMD dropped the 1200 hp SW1200 and replaced it with the 1500 hp SW 1500.

(Above) Some of the PC SW1500's have a history very similar to the 2000 series ex PRSL GP38's. Five brand new SW1500's were delivered in Indiana Harbor Belt RR paint in November 1970. Suddenly, that week the banking community deemed the credit worthiness of the subsidiary unsatisfactory, but remarkably parent Penn Central's was good enough to assume ownership of the orphaned units. The units were quickly

relettered PC and except for the white frame stripe, have nothing to show for their very short tenure as IHB locomotives. 9227 is pictured at Chicago, 1/24/71.

(Below) A more normal purchase by Penn Central in 1972 led to this SW1500, #9513, pictured at the passenger car shops at Harmon, N.Y. September 1974. Note the "Car Trak" plate underneath the last "N" in Penn. The plate was an industry-wide attempt to read car and locomotive data electronically as they entered yards. It died an early death in the seventies and is now just another part of our railroad history.

R.J. Yanosey

S 1
9300 - 9499

M.S. Zak Collection

The S1 was a 660 hp switcher manufactured by Alco-GE from 1940-1950. The 539 engined, S1 was a solid performer and sold well to all three PC predecessors.

(Top) PC 9336 was an ex NYC S1 shown at Camden 10/10/70. Note the jaunty headlite visor that some NYC units wore.

(Center) 9422 was an ex NH S1 at Camden 10/3/70. The lettering under the number reads: "R.I. 5094 owned by a bank or trust co. under security agreement filed under Interstate Commerce Act Sect. 20C."

(Below) S1 9437 at Camden 9/18/71 was an ex PRR unit manufactured in March 1949.

M.S. Zak Collection

M.S. Zak Collection

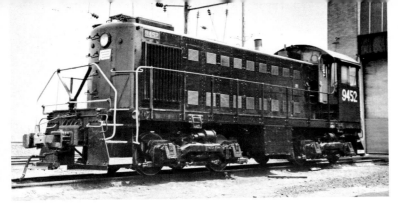

M.S. Zak Collection

Ex Pennsy S1's illustrate two methods to paint a diesel "Penn Central":

(Left) PC 9452 built in early 1949 is completely black with minimal identification, just a worm on the nose and a number under the cab window. If it was not an FRA regulation to paint the handrails and end steps yellow, the unit would be a virtual "dip" job. Photographed at Morrisville 4/30/72.

(Center) S1 9461 shown at Kearny Meadows, N.J. July 1975 shows the paint scheme carried by most Alco switchers on Penn Central. The name was spelled out on the long hood but the radiator prevented the usual PC logo placement.

(Below) PC S1 9496 switches a five car cut out of South Station Boston on May 25, 1969. These ex NH S1's are unique in having flattened cab roofs to allow for extra clearance in overhead electric territory

M.S. Zak Collection

R.J. Yanosey

220

RJ Yanosey

M.S. Zak Collection

S2
9600-9860

The S2 was the big switcher offered by Alco-GE during the same 1940-50 decade spanned by the 660 hp S1. The S2 also had six cylinders in its 539 engine but produced 1000 hp thanks to a turbocharger which, of course, the S1 lacked. Purchased by all three roads most of the veteran units served successfully throughout Penn Central's ownership.

PC 9717 (top) was an earlier S2 manufactured in January 1945 and is shown at Morrisville 4/1/72, just over 27 years old. The veteran's headlite is eye catching not only because of the NYC visor, but because of its smallness and high placement.

(2nd from top) PC 9731 is also an ex NYC S2, manufactured in August 1948, but with a twin sealed beam headlite added sometime after it had left the Alco plant. It is pictured awaiting disposition by Conrail (scrapping), at Croxton Yard (former EL) Secaucus, N.J. in August 1977. Very, very few PC Alco switchers saw CR lettering.

(3rd from top) PC 9780 shown at Harsimus Cove, Jersey City, N.J. one month before Conrail in March 1976 was a former PRR S2 built in 1949. Both the S1 and S2 can be picked out by their "Blunt" trucks.

(Bottom) 9857 was a former NH S2 built with that road's optioned flat roof. In this photo, the unit has had its PC markings painted out and stenciled for GE, its ultimate destination as trade in material. Shown at Morrisville, Pa. 7/77. Conrail kept the Alco switchers about a year to get itself over the usual post merger power crunch, and then purged itself of the breed.

RJ Yanosey

RJ Yanosey

R.J. Yanosey

(Above) The tired Blunts of PC 9804 rest on a weekend in April 1973 at the Hunter Produce Yard in Newark, N.J. For many years reefers from Florida and California would fill this yard as trucks from nearby foodstores would pull up and offload vegetables and fruit in crates and burlap bags. The cobble stones have undoubtedly been doused with the brine of thousands of reefers, but in 1973 simply bear up a weary ex PRR S2.

(Below) About 5 miles east of Newark, the Kearny Meadows Shops plays host to several Alco switchers on a hot summer night in July 1971. Fifteen years later, the Alcos would be long gone and the shop would be demolished for construction of a new locomotive/MU facility for NJ Transit.

R.J. Yanosey

M.S. Zak Collection

By early 1950, Alco had reworked the S1 and reintroduced its 660 hp unit as the S3. Also using the 539 engine, externally the S3 differed with the S1 by the use of AAR type A trucks. By this time NH was about finished with its steam replacement program and never purchased the S3, while NYC and PRR did.

(Above) PC S3 9400 was the NYC 898 before the merger. It was manufactured in August 1950 and is shown here at Philadelphia October 4, 1970.

(Below) S3 9475 was the former PRR 8875, a November 1950 Alco-GE product. It is pictured here at Camden October 17, 1970.

S3
9348-9485

R. J. Yanosey

S4
9601-9834

Like its S3 counterpart, Alco replaced the 1000 hp S2 in 1950 with the new S4. The S4 also rode on AAR type A trucks instead of Blunts, and likewise sold to PRR and NYC but not the New Haven.

(Top) PC 9729 was an ex NYC S4 built in the spring of 1952 and shown here awaiting Conrail disposition at Frontier Yard, Buffalo in April 1977.

D. Harnley, Herbert H. Harwood Collection

(2nd from top) PC 9741 is an ex NYC ex P&LE S4 at Seneca Yard outside Buffalo, July 1974. Note the difference in positioning of the headlites on 9729 and 9741.

(3rd from top) PC 9800 was the former PRR 8900 before the merger. The S4 is shown in the Kearny Meadows in May 1975.

R. J. Yanosey

(Bottom) PC 9833 was an ex PRR S4 built in January 1954. Shown here at Kearny in May 1976.

R. J. Yanosey

HH660
9411

E.D. Galvin, Herbert H. Harwood Collection

R.J. Yanosey

Just before S1 production began in 1940, Alco offered a 660 hp switcher powered by its 539 (May 1939) engine. This was the HH660. Penn Central inherited New Haven's sole remaining example, #924 and renumbered it 9411. Built in January 1940, the locomotive just kept running and so there was simply no reason to scrap it, even though it was 30 years of age in 1970. Something uncommon for a class 1 railroad to own in 1970, the 9411 even had a PC logo applied over its NH paint during the 1970-71 PC'ing campaign. It finally was scrapped in 1971. (Above) HH660 9411 at Dover Street, Boston February 1970 was the oldest Alco to operate for Penn Central.

T6
9844 - 9849

In March 1958, Pennsy purchased a half dozen of the 251 powered, Alco T6. An example of the relatively rare 1000 hp unit is 9849 shown (above) at Phillipsburg, N.J. 4/74.

(Right) The view from Bridge Street in Metuchen, N.J. June 11, 1977 shows overhead detail on the 9848. The T in T6 stands for Transfer, and the units had transition control for this type work, something lacking in regular switchers.

D.T. Walker

225

R.J. Yanosey

RS1
9900 - 9946

Often thought of as the first roadswitchers, the RS1 was technically just a switcher with a longer frame and short hood. Regardless, the 1000 hp unit saw a multitude of duties after being purchased by all three predecessors. PC inherited some from each road but the original group was cut by a third by continual retirement of these classic diesels.

(Top) PC 9904 was a NYC purchase of early 1948. It had been sitting dead for some time when this photo was taken in May 1977 at Morrisville. Ex NH models looked exactly the same except for a distinct extended cab roof or "lip" on either end that was used as a sun visor.

(Center) PC 9915 was an ex PRR RS1 manufactured relatively late in May 1952. One of the "best dressed" PC RS1's, the 9915 was in between switching assignments at Hays Avenue, Newark, N.J. May 1976 when this photo was taken.

(Below) PC RS1 9917 tacks an N5 caboose onto the rear of a westbound freight in the Meadows Yard, Kearny, N.J. August 1973.

R.J. Yanosey

R.J. Yanosey

DL600m
9949

In 1975, PC decided to experiment and take its successful RS3/EMD program one step further by repowering a DL600B. The 6811 was chosen to receive an EMD 1200 hp prime mover and to be coupled to a slug made out of RSD5 6803(2). Apparently too close to Conrail to warrant duplication, the single attempt (both units renumbered 9949) spent its entire career on the hump at DeWitt Yard, Syracuse, NY. (right) March 1976.

RS3m
9950 - 9984

T. Trencansky, Herbert H. Harwood Collection

Well satisfied with its RS3 repowering program, Penn Central decided to renumber the several rebuilt RS3m's scattered in the 5000 series and start a continuous block at 9950. (Below) The second rebuild, low nose 9951, the former 5230, switches the Baltimore piggyback terminal in November 1974.

Herbert H. Harwood

Herbert H. Harwood, RJY Collection

"No Nose" 9950 was certainly a unique diesel, created by the shop forces of Penn Central. While there have been RS3 repowerings similar to the other "normal" nose RS3m's of PC, 9950 the former 5477, has never been duplicated anywhere.

Switching at Baltimore in April 1974, above, with the long hood forward it appears quite normal. After all this is the "F" end. Turned around, however, like the photo below at the B&O interchange in Baltimore in October 1975, the distinctive 9950 was certainly a breed apart.

Herbert H. Harwood

The RS3m program adopted a more normal pattern after the no frills 9950 and extra frills 9951, by simply leaving well enough alone on the RS3m short hood. After these two, PC went on to build over 30 more RS3m's such as 9962 at Brewster, N.Y. (top) in May 1976, and (center) 9963 at Buffalo April 1977. The lucky RS3's chosen to be rebuilt would go on to see about 7 extra years of life compared to unrebuilt RS3's, finally succumbing to Conrail scrapping in 1985. Some, happily, were sold to shortlines and saw further service.

R. J. Yanosey

R. J. Yanosey

GE 44 ton
9999

Taking advantage of a labor agreement which allowed a diesel under 45 tons to operate without a fireman, Pennsy ordered a small fleet of GE 44 ton switchers in the late 1940's to replace small 0-4-0 steam switchers. Not too successful because of their light weight, only one 44 tonner would survive to take title to the very end of the PC roster. PC 9999 shown here at Camden in October 1976, held down the same job on the Union Transportation shortline, that the final PRR steamer, B6sb 5244, an 0-6-0, held.

R. J. Yanosey

229

PENN CENTRAL ALL-TIME LOCOMOTIVE ROSTER
By Mark S. Branibar

Locomotive Number	Model	Previous History	Notes	Locomotive Number	Model	Previous History	Notes
15	SW8	DESPATCH SHOPS, INC.	7	1663,-1666, 1670-1672	F7A	NYC 1663-1666, 1670-1672	5
712	F7B	D&RGW 5712	8	1674, 1675, 1677-1679	F7A	NYC 1674, 1675, 1677-1679	
721	F7A	D&RGW 5721	8	1681-1697, 1698	F7A	NYC 1681-1684, 1686-1697	
733	F7B	D&RGW 5733	8	1698, 1701-1707	F7A	NYC 1698 (2ND), 1701-1707	5
754	F7A	D&RGW 5754	8	1709-1712, 1714-1716	F7A	NYC 1709-1712, 1714-1716	5
1009	FA1	NYC 1009		1718, 1719, 1721, 1722	F7A	NYC 1718, 1719, 1721, 1722	
1044, 1045, 1049-1055	FA2	NYC 1044, 1045, 1049-1055		1724-1735, 1739, 1742-	F7A	NYC 1724-1735, 1739, 1742-	5
1060, 1061, 1063, 1067-	FA2	NYC 1060, 1061, 1063, 1067-		1750, 1752-1768, 1770-	F7A	1750, 1752-1768, 1770-	5
1071, 1073-1076, 1080-	FA2	1071, 1073-1076, 1080-		1776, 1778, 1779, 1781-	F7A	1776, 1778, 1779, 1781-	
1084, 1086, 1087, 1089	FA2	1084, 1086, 1087, 1089		1785, 1787-1793, 1795-	F7A	1785, 1787-1793, 1795-	5
1091, 1098, 1099, 1102-	FA2	NYC 1091, 1098, 1099, 1102-		1798, 1802-1804, 1807	F7A	1798, 1802-1804, 1807	
1104, 1108, 1109	FA2	1104, 1108, 1109		1808, 1810-1817, 1820	F7A	NYC 1808, 1810-1817, 1820	
1110	FA1	NYC 1110 (2ND)		1821, 1824-1826, 1828	F7A	NYC 1821, 1824-1826, 1828	
1111-1113	FA2	NYC 1111-1113		1829, 1831-1835, 1837	F7A	NYC 1829, 1831-1835, 1837	
1119	FA1	NYC 1119 (2ND)		1839-1842, 1845, 1847-	F7A	NYC 1839-1842, 1845, 1847-	5
1120, 1122	FA2	NYC 1120, 1122		1856, 1858, 1860, 1862-	F7A	1856, 1858, 1860, 1862-	
1300	FA1	PC 1009		1866, 1870-1872	F7A	1866, 1870-1872	
1302, 1304, 1308-	FA2	PC 1102, 1104, 1108-	9	1878, 1879	F7A	PC 721, 754	12
1311, 1313	FA2	1111, 1113		1903-1905, 1906	F7A	PRR 9659A-9661A, 9666A	11
1319	FA1	PC 1119		2010-2014	GP38	NEW 7, 8/70	1, 13
1330-1333	FA1	NH 0401, 0418, 0426, 0428	9	2021-2044	RS32	NYC 8021-8044	
1345, 1349-1351, 1354	FA2	PC 1045, 1049-1051, 1054	5	2050-2059	C430	NYC 2050-2059	14
1355, 1361, 1369, 1371	FA2	PC 1055, 1061, 1069, 1071		2100-2105, 2106	GP20	NYC 6100-6105, 6107	
1373, 1375, 1376, 1380-	FA2	PC 1073, 1075, 1076, 1080-		2107, 2108-2112	GP20	NYC 6108, 6110-6114	5
1384, 1386, 1389, 1391	FA2	1084, 1086, 1089, 1091		2188-2197	GP30	NYC 6115-6124	5
1398, 1399	FA2	PC 1098, 1099		2198, 2199, 2200-2249	GP30	NYC 6125, 6126, 2200-2249	5
1403, 1408, 1410,	F3A	PRR 9530A, 9541A, 9550A	10	2198, 2199, 2200-2249	GP30	PRR 2250, 2251, 2200-2249	5
1416, 1419, 1420	F3A	PRR 9561A, 9677A, 9683A		2250, 2251, 2252-2308	GP35	PRR 2309, 2310, 2252-2308	5
1422, 1423	F3A	PRR 9685A, 9686A		2309, 2310, 2311-2351	GP35	PRR 2369, 2370, 2311-2351	5
1440, 1442, 1443	F7A	PRR 9640A, 9643A, 9644A		2353-2368	GP35	PRR 2353-2368	5
1444, 1450, 1451	F7A	PRR 9646A, 9654A, 9662A	11	2369-2383, 2385-2399	GP35	NYC 6125-6139, 6141-6155	5, 15
1454, 1455, 1457	F7A	PRR 9667A, 9668A, 9670A		2400-2414	RS27 (DL640)	PRR 2400-2414	5
1458, 1464, 1469	F7A	PRR 9673A, 9697A, 9768A		2415	C424	PRR 2415	16
1472, 1473, 1475	F7A	PRR 9771A, 9772A, 9774A		2416-2446	C425	PRR 2416-2446	5
1476, 1477, 1478	F7A	PRR 9775A, 9777A, 9778A		2450-2459	C425	NH 2550-2559	
1481, 1482, 1485	F7A	PRR 9781A, 9782A, 9785A	11	2500-2569	U25B	NYC 2500-2569	17
1488, 1490, 1491	F7A	PRR 9788A, 9790A, 9791A		2600-2648, 2649-2658	U25B	PRR 2500-2548, 2649-2658	5, 18
1494, 1497, 1500	F7A	PRR 9794A, 9797A, 9800A		2660-2685	U25B	NH 2500-2525	19
1501, 1503, 1505	F7A	PRR 9801A, 9803A, 9805A	11	2700-2749	U23B	NEW 8-10/72	1
1509, 1511, 1514	F7A	PRR 9809A, 9811A, 9814A		2750-2776	U23B	NEW 8-10/73	1, 20
1517, 1520, 1523	F7A	PRR 9817A, 9820A, 9823A		(2809-2811)	U28B	P&LE 2809-2811	3
1524, 1527, 1530	F7A	PRR 9824A, 9827A, 9830A		2822, 2823	U28B	NYC 2822, 2823	
1531, 1533, 1537	F7A	PRR 9831A, 9874A, 9878A		2830-2857	U30B	NYC 2830-2857	
1538	F7A	PRR 9879A		2858, 2859	U33B	NYC 2858, 2859	21
1617, 1619, 1633, 1635	F3A	NYC 1617, 1619, 1633, 1635		2860-2889	U30B	NYC 2860-2889	22
1637, 1639, 1641, 1642	F7A	NYC 1637, 1639, 1641, 1642		2890-2955	U33B	NEW 9-12/68	1
1644, 1646, 1648, 1650	F7A	NYC 1644, 1646, 1648, 1650	5	2956-2970	U33B	NEW 5, 6/70	1, 23
1651, 1656, 1657, 1659	F7A	NYC 1651, 1656, 1657, 1659	5	3000-3104	GP40	NYC 3000-3104	5, 24
				3105-3259	GP40	NEW 8-12/68	1, 6

230

Locomotive Number	Model	Previous History	Notes	Locomotive Number	Model	Previous History	Notes
3260-3274	GP40	EMD 11-20, 22-26	2	4283, 4284-4293	E8A	PRR 5803A, 5884A-5893A	5, 26
3323-3325, 3327, 3328	FB2	NYC 3323-3325, 3327, 3328		4294-4299, 4300	E8A	PRR 5894-5899, 5700A	28
3330, 3331, 3337, 3338	FB2	NYC 3330, 3331, 3337, 3338		4301-4305	E8A	PRR 5801A, 5902-5905	
3341, 3342, 3345, 3346	FB2	NYC 3341, 3342, 3345, 3346		4306, 4307, 4308-	E8A	PRR 5806A, 5807A, 5808-	5, 29
3348, 3350, 3355-3358	FB2	NYC 3348, 3350, 3355-3358		4310, 4311-4316	E8A	5810, 5711A-5716A	
3362, 3364, 3365, 3367	FB2	NYC 3362, 3364, 3365, 3367		4317-4319	E8A	PRR 5835, 5838, 5839	
3368	FB1	NYC 3368 (2ND)		4320-4323	E8A	PC 4068, 4070, 4071, 4076	30
3370, 3372	FB2	NYC 3370, 3372		4324-4328	E8A	PC 4079, 4080, 4083-4085	30
3390-3392	FB1	NH 0456, 0458, 0462		4332-4371	FP7A	PRR 9832A-9871A	5
3393-3397	FB2	NH 0465-0469		4400-4457	E44	PRR 4400-4457	5
3429, 3432, 3437, 3438	F7B	NYC 2429, 2432, 2437, 2438		4458-4465	E44A	PRR 4458-4465	
3439-3442	F7B	NYC 2439-2442		4600-4610	E33	NH 300-310	
3444, 3449-3456, 3458	F3B	NYC 2444, 2449-2456, 2458		4622	P-2A	NYC 222	
3460-3462, 3464, 3466-	F3B	NYC 2460-2462, 2464, 2466-		4623-4642	P-2B	NYC 223-242	
3469, 3471, 3473	F3B	2469, 2471, 2473		4655	T-1A	NYC 255	
3478, 3479	F7B	PC 712, 733	12	4662	T-2A	NYC 262	
3505	F3B	PRR 9545		4663, 4666, 4667	T-2B	NYC 263, 266, 267	
3508, 3512, 3516	F7B	PRR 9547B, 9641B, 9645B		4669, 4671	T-2B	NYC 269, 271	
3521, 3525, 3526	F7B	PRR 9652B, 9660B, 9668B		4673-4676, 4678-4680	T-3A	NYC 273-276, 278-280	
3528, 3541, 3544	F7B	PRR 9672B, 9782B, 9788B		4702, 4705, 4708, 4710	S-2	NYC 102, 105, 108, 110	
3546-3548	F7B	PRR 9792B, 9794B, 9796B	11	4715, 4718, 4723-4725	S-2	NYC 115, 118, 123-125	
3554-3556	F7B	PRR 9808B, 9810B, 9812B		4727, 4730-4733	S-2	NYC 127, 130-133	
3557, 3560, 3561	F7B	PRR 9814B, 9872B, 9874B		4751, 4752, 4754	B-1	PRR 3912, 3913, 5685	
3562, 3563	F7B	PRR 9876B, 9878B		4755-4757	B-1	PRR 5687, 5690, 5693	
3800-3829	GP9B	PRR 7175B-7204B	5	4780, 4781	DD-1	PRR 3936, 3937	
3830-3839	GP9B	PRR 7230B-7239B		4790	L-6	PRR 5939	
4001, 4002	E7	NYC 4001, 4002		4791	L-6A	PRR 5940	
4003	E8Am	NYC 4003	25	4800-4803, 4806, 4808-	GG1	PRR 4800-4803, 4806, 4808-	
4005-4008, 4010	E7A	NYC 4005-4008, 4010		4811, 4815, 4816, 4818	GG1	4811, 4815, 4816, 4818	
4011, 4012, 4014	E7A	NYC 4011, 4012, 4014		4821, 4822, 4824-4828	GG1	PRR 4821, 4822, 4824-4828	
4015, 4018, 4019	E7A	NYC 4015, 4018, 4019		4832, 4835-4842, 4844	GG1	PRR 4832, 4835-4842, 4844	
4020	E8Am	NYC 4020	25	4845, 4848-4870	GG1	PRR 4845, 4848-4870	5
4021-4035	E7A	NYC 4021-4035		4872-4887, 4889-4929	GG1	PRR 4872-4887,4889-4929	5,31,32
4036-4076, 4078-4085	E8A	NYC 4036-4076, 4078-4085		4930-4938 (1ST)	GG1	PRR 4930-4938	5
4087-4095	E8A	NYC 4087-4095		4930-4932 (2ND)	GG1	PC 4904, 4905, 4909	
4100-4113	E7B	NYC 4100-4113		4933-4934 (2ND)	GG1	PC 4915, 4917	
4114	E7B	PRR 5900B		4935	GG1	PC 4935	
4115-4126	E7B	PRR 5840B-5862B EVEN #		4936-4938 (2ND)	GG1	PC 4921-4923	
4151	F7B	PRR 9834B		4939	GG1	PC 4927	
4153-4159	F7B	PRR 9838B-9850B EVEN #		4970-4977	E40	NH 371-377, 379	
4200, 4201	E7A	PRR 5900, 5901		5000-5059	FL9	NH 2000-2059	33,34,35
4202, 4203, 4204	E7A	PRR 5882A, 5883A, 5880A		5100-5107, 5109-5112	H16-44	NYC 7000-7007, 7009-7012	
4205, 4206	E7A	PRR 5881A, 5846A		5158	H16-44	PRR 8815	36
4208-4214, 4216	E7A	PRR 5848A-5854A, 5856A		5160-5174	H16-44	NH 1600-1614	
4217, 4219-4221	E7A	PRR 5857A, 5859A-5861A		5203, 5205	RS3	NYC 8203(2ND), 8205(2ND)	
4223-4235	E7A	PRR 5863A-5875A		5207, 5210, 5212, 5215	RS2	NYC 8207, 8210, 8212, 8215	
4237-4239	E7A	PRR 5877A-5879A		5223, 5224, 5227	RS3	NYC 8223, 8224, 8227	
4240-4245	E7A	PRR 5840A-5845A		5221	RS2	NYC8221	
4246, 4247	E8A	PRR 5836, 5837	5	5227 (2ND)	RS3m	PC 5227	39
4248-4259, 4260-	E8A	PRR 5788A-5799A,5760A-	5,26,27	5228	RS3	NYC 8228	
4269, 4270, 4271-	E8A	5769A, 5805A, 5701A-		5229	RS2	NYC 8229 (2ND)	
4280, 4281, 4282	E8A	5710A, 5804A, 5802A		5230	RS3	NYC 8230	

231

Locomotive Number	Model	Previous History	Notes	Locomotive Number	Model	Previous History	Notes
5230 (2ND)	RS3m	PC 5230	38	5546, 5547, 5549-5553	RS3	PRR 8846, 8847, 8849-8853	42
5231-5234, 5235	RS3	NYC 8231-8234, 8235 (2ND)		5554	RS3	NH 531	42
5236-5240	RS3	NYC 8236-8240		5555, 5557, 5558	RS3	PRR 8855, 8903, 8905	42
5240 (2ND)	RS3m	PC 5240	39	5559	RS3	NH 532	42
5241, 5242	RS3	NYC 8241, 8242		5560	RS3	PRR 8910	42
5242 (2ND)	RS3m	PC 5242	40	5561	RS3	NH 533	42
5243, 5246	RS3	NYC 8243, 8246		5562	RS3	PRR 8912	42
5256	RS3	PC 5525 (1ST)		5564	RS3	NH 536	42
5257	RS3	NYC 8257		5565	RS3	PRR 8915	42
5258	RS3	PC 5526 (1ST)		5566	RS3	NH 539	42
5260, 5262, 5263, 5272	RS3	NYC 8260, 8262, 8263, 8272		5567-5569	RS3	PRR 8443-8445	42
5282, 5287, 5288, 5290	RS3	NYC 8282, 8287, 8288, 8290		5569 (2ND)	RS2	LV 211 (1ST)	42, 43
5292-5295, 5297-5299	RS3	NYC 8292-8295, 8297-8299		5570	RS3	NH 540	42
5301, 5302-5320	RS3	NYC 8301 (2ND), 8302-8320		5571-5584	RS3	PRR 8471-8484	42
5322, 5323, 5325-5330	RS3	NYC 8322, 8323, 8325-8330		5585-5588, 5589-5591	RS3	NH 541-544, 546, 549, 551	6,42
5332, 5333, 5336, 5339	RS3	NYC 8332, 8333, 8336, 8339		5592-5595, 5596-5598	RS3	NH 553-556, 559-561	42
5340, 5342, 5343, 5345	RS3	NYC 8340, 8342, 8343, 8345		5600-5607, 5609, 5611	GP7	NYC 5600-5607, 5609, 5611	44
5346, 5348-5352	RS3	NYC 8346, 8348-8352		5612-5619	GP7	NYC (P&E) 5612-5619	
5360-5362	RS3	PC 5538, 5540, 5542		5620	GP7	NYC (P&E) 5620 (2ND)	
5363-5365	RS3	PC 5546, 5547, 5581		5621-5625	GP7	NYC (P&E) 5621-5625	
5400-5401	RS3	PRR 8600-8601		5626-5630, 5631	GP7	NYC 5626-5630, 5631 (2ND)	
5401 (2ND)	RS2	LV 212 (1ST)	41	5632-5670	GP7	NYC 5632-5670	
5402-5405, 5409, 5411	RS3	PRR 8602-8605, 8909, 8592		5670 (2ND)	GP7	PC 5763	
5413, 5414, 5415, 5416	RS3	PRR 8903, 8904, 8435, 8436		5671, 5672	GP7	NYC 5671, 5672 (2ND)	
5418, 5419	RS3	PRR 8818, 8819		5673-5675, 5687-5712	GP7	NYC 5673-5675, 5687-5712	
5419 (2ND)	RS3	PC 5447 (1ST)		5719	GP7	P&LE 5719	
5420-5422, 5424	RS3	PRR 8820-8822, 8824		5738-5752	GP7	NYC 5738-5752	
5424 (2ND)	RS3	PC 5419 (1ST)		5752 (2ND)	GP7	PC 5757	
5425-5428, 5430-5433	RS3	PRR 8825-8828, 8830-8833		5754-5757, 5759-5761	GP7	NYC 5754-5757, 5759-5761	
5435, 5436, 5437-5442	RS3	PRR 8835, 8836, 8437-8442		5763	GP7	PC 7519	
5443-5447	RS3	PRR 8593-8597		5764	GP7	NYC 5764	
5447 (2ND)	RS3	PC 5424 (1ST)		5766, 5768-5770	GP7	PC 5904, 5906-5908	
5448, 5449, 5450	RS3	PRR 8598, 8599, 8590	5	5772, 5773, 5775	GP7	PC 5910, 5911, 5913	
5451, 5452-5461	RS3	PRR 8591, 8452-8461	41	5776-5778, 5780, 5781	GP7	NYC 5776-5778, 5780, 5781	
5461 (2ND)	RS2	LV 210 (1ST)		5783	GP7	PC 5915	
5462-5470	RS3	PRR 8462-8470		5786, 5788	GP7	NYC 5786, 5788	
5471, 5472, 5473, 5474	RS3	NH 517, 520, 523, 527		5789, 5790	GP7	PC 5918, 5919	
5475, 5476, 5477	RS3	NH 528, 534, 535		5792, 5793	GP7	NYC 5792, 5793	
5477 (2ND)	RS3m	PC 5477	37	5794, 5795	GP7	PC 5921, 5922	
5478, 5479, 5480, 5481	RS3	NH 537, 538, 545, 547		5800	GP7	NYC 5800	
5482, 5483, 5484	RS3	NH 548, 557, 558		5801	GP7	PC 5925	
5485, 5487, 5488	RS3	PC 5559, 5595, 5591		5802-5805	GP7	NYC 5802-5805	
5500, 5501-5504, 5505	RS3	NYC 8247, 8252-8255, 8259	42	5807	GP7	PC 5927	
5506-5513, 5514-5521	RS3	NYC 8264-8271, 8273-8280	42	5808-5812	GP7	NYC 5808-5812	
5522-5524	RS3	NYC 8248, 8250, 8251	42	5816	GP7	PC 7369	
5525, 5526	RS3	NYC 8256, 8258	42	5818-5827	GP7	NYC 5818-5827	45
5525-5526 (2ND)	RS3	NH 518, 519	42	5840-5844, 5845, 5846	GP7	PRR 8800-8804, 8545, 8546	
5527-5530	RS3	NYC 8285, 8286, 8289, 8291	42	5847-5850, 5852, 5853	GP7	PRR 8547-8550, 8502, 8503	
5531-5533	RS3	NH 521, 522, 524	42	5854-5857	GP7	PRR 8554-8557	
5534-5536	RS3	NH 525, 526, 529	42	5857 (2ND)	GP7	PC 5885 (1ST)	
5537-5540, 5542-5544	RS3	PRR 8837-8840, 8842-8844	42	5858-5882	GP7	PRR 8558-8582	
5544 (2ND)	RS3	NH 530	42	5882 (2ND)	GP7	PC 5887 (1ST)	

Locomotive Number	Model	Previous History	Notes
5884	GP7	PRR 8504	
5884 (2ND)	GP7	PC 5850	
5885	GP7	PRR 8505	
5885 (2ND)	GP7	PC 5857 (1ST)	
5886	GP7	PRR 8506	
5886 (2ND)	GP7	PC 5862	
5887	GP7	PRR 8507	
5887 (2ND)	GP7	PC 5882 (1ST)	
5888	GP7	PRR 8508	
5888 (2ND)	GP7	PC 5864	
5889-5892	GP7	PRR 8509-8512	
5893, 5894	GP7	PC 5954 (1ST), 5950	
5895, 5896, 5897-5899	GP7	PRR 8805, 8806, 8797-8799	
5900, 5902, 5903-5913	GP7	NYC 5753, 5762, 5765-5775	42
5914-5917, 5918-5920	GP7	NYC 5782-5785,5789-5791	42, 46
5921-5924	GP7	NYC 5794, 5795, 5797, 5799	42
5925-5927	GP7	NYC 5801, 5806, 5807	42
5950, 5951, 5952-5954	GP7	PRR 8500, 8501, 8551-8553	42
5954 (2ND)	GP7	PC 5951	42
5955-5959	GP7	PRR 8583-8587	42
6000-6039	SD35	PRR 6000-6039	5
6040-6104	SD40	PRR 6040-6104	5, 17, 47
6105-6234	SD45	PRR 6105-6234	5,48,49,50
6235-6239	SD45	NEW 8/68	1
6240-6284	SD40	NEW 12/70-2/71	1
6300-6314	C628	PRR 6300-6314	5, 17
6315-6329	C630	PRR 6315-6329	
6330-6344	C636	NEW 2-4/68	1
6500-6519	U25C	PRR 6500-6519	50
6520-6534	U28C	PRR 6520-6534	
6535-6539	U30C	PRR 6535-6539	
6540-6559	U33C	NEW 2-4/68	1, 5, 51
6560-6563	U33C	NEW 8/68	1
6700-6708	H24-66	PRR 8700-8707, 8699	
6700-6708 (2ND)	U23C	NEW 10/70	1
6709-6718	U23C	NEW 10-11/70	1
6799	H24-66	PC 6700	
6800-6803	RSD5	PRR 8446-8449	
6803 (2ND)	RSD5	PC 6804 (1ST)	52
6804	RSD5	PRR 8450	
6804 (2ND)	RSD5	PC 6803 (1ST)	52
6805	RSD5	PRR 8451	
6806-6810	RSD7	PRR 8606-8610	5
6811-6816	RSD15	PRR 8611-8616	5
6855-6879	RSD12	PRR 8655-8679	5
6900-6924	SD9	PRR 7600-7624	5, 53
6950 & 6951 (1ST)	SD7	PRR 8588, 8589	
6925-6959	SD38	NEW 4/70	1, 54
6966, 6967	AS616	PRR 8966, 8967	
6973-6976	AS616	PRR 8973, 8974, 8111, 8112	
6998, 6999	SD7	PC 6950 & 6951 (1ST)	
7000-7070, 7072-7128	GP9	PRR 7000-7070, 7072-7128	5
7130-7224, 7226-7269	GP9	PRR 7130-7224, 7226-7269	5
7271, 7272, 7277	GP9	PC7531, 7532, 7537	
7280 7281, 7284	GP9	PC 7540, 7541, 7544	
7286	GP9	NH 1216	
7290-7293, 7298	GP9	PC 7550-7553, 7558	
7300-7303	GP9	NYC (CUT) 5900-5903	42
7304-7314, 7316-7320	GP9	NYC 5904-5914, 5916-5920	
7322-7327	GP9	NYC 5922-5927	
7329, 7331, 7332, 7335	GP9	PC 7501, 7503, 7504, 7507	
7337-7339, 7343, 7344	GP9	PC 7509-7511, 7515, 7516	
7346	GP9	NYC 5946	
7347	GP9	PC 7518	
7348	GP7	NYC 5948 (2ND)	
7349-7359, 7361-7364	GP9	NYC 5949-5959, 5961-5964	
7366-7368	GP9	NYC 5966-5968	
7369	GP7	NYC 5969 (2ND)	
7371-7379	GP9	NYC 5971-5979	
7380	GP7	NYC 5980 (2ND)	
7381-7419	GP9	NYC 5981-6019	5
7420	GP7	NYC 6020 (2ND)	
7421-7441, 7443-7451	GP9	NYC 6021-6041,6043-6051	5,45
7452	GP7	NYC 6052 (2ND)	
7453-7463, 7465	GP9	NYC 6053-6063, 6065	
7468-7475	GP9	NYC 6068-6075	
7500-7504, 7506-7508	GP9	NYC 5928-5932,5934-59365	,42
7510-7512	GP9	NYC 5938-5940	42
7514-7518	GP9	NYC 5942-5945, 5947	
7519	GP7	NYC 5948 (2ND)	42
7530-7536,7538-7545	GP9	NH1200-1206,1208-1215	42
7547-7559	GP9	NH 1217-1229	42
7600-7608	RS11	NYC 8000-8008	
7617-7639, 7645-7647	RS11	PRR 8617-8639, 8645-8647	5
7649-7654	RS11	PRR 8649-8654	
7660-7674	RS11	NH 1400-1414	
7675-7799	GP38	NEW 6-11/69	1, 55
7800, 7801, 7803, 7804	DS44-660	PRR 9220, 9001, 9003, 9004	
7805, 7807, 7808, 7809	DS44-660	PRR 9005, 9007, 9008, 9029	
7810, 7811, 7815, 7816	DS44-660	PRR 9110, 9111, 9115, 9116	
7818, 7819, 7820, 7821	DS44-660	PRR 9118, 9019, 9120, 9121	
7823, 7826, 7827, 7828	DS44-660	PRR 9223, 9226, 9027, 9228	
7832, 7833-7836	DS44-660	PRR 9232, 9233-9236	
7837-7841, 7842	DS44-660	PRR 9037-9041, 9023	
7843, 7845, 7847, 7848	DS44-660	PRR 9043, 9025, 9036, 9048	
7849-7852	DS44-660	PRR 9049, 9020-9022	
7853, 7856, 7860-7862	DS44-660	PRR 9013, 9016, 5960-5962	
7864, 7865, 7866, 7867	DS44-660	PRR 5964, 9221, 5966, 9024	
7869	DS44-660	PC 7809 (1ST)	
7870, 7871	DS44-660	PRR 9210, 9211	
7871 (2ND)	DS44-660	PC 7801 (1ST)	
7872 & 7873	DS44-660	PRR 9212, 9213	
7872 & 7873 (2ND)	DS44-660	PC 7815 (1ST), 7803 (1ST)	
7875, 7876	DS44-660	PRR 9215, 9216	

Locomotive Number	Model	Previous History	Notes
7877, 7879,7880	DS44-660	PC 7820 ,7821, 7810 (1ST)	
7881, 7882	DS44-660	PRR 9031, 9032	
7883, 7885	DS44-660	PC 7816 (1ST), 7805 (1ST)	
7886, 7887, 7889	DS44-750	PRR 5596, 5617, 5599	
7890-7893	DS44-750	PRR 5616, 5611-5613	
7896, 7898	S-8	PRR 8996, 8998	
7900-7902, 7904	DS44-750	PRR 5614, 5615, 5602, 5604	
7906, 7908, 7910, 7911	DS44-750	PRR 5606, 5608, 5610, 5595	
7912, 7913	DS44-750	PRR 5597, 5600	
7916-7921, 7924, 7926	DS44-1000	PRR 9266-9271, 9263, 9126	
7928, 7930, 7932, 7935	DS44-1000	PRR 9128, 9130, 9132, 9135	
7938-7943, 7945-7947	DS44-1000	PRR 5968-5873, 5975-5977	
7948, 7950, 7952	DS44-1000	PRR 9273, 5550, 5551	
7953-7957, 7959-7961	DS44-1000	PRR 5553-5557, 5559-5561	
7963-7971, 7973-7976	DS44-1000	PRR 5563-5571, 5573-5576	
7978, 7980, 7981, 7985	DS44-1000	PRR 5578, 5580, 5581, 5585	
7986-7991	DS44-1000	PRR 5586-5590, 9251	
7995-7998	DS44-1000	PRR 9255-9257, 9178	
7999, 8001, 8003, 8004	DS44-1000	PRR 9179, 9051, 9053, 9054	
8006-8008, 8010	DS44-1000	PRR 9054, 9056-9058, 9060	
8012-8016	DS44-1000	PRR 9062-9066	
8017-8020	DS44-1000	PRR 9272, 9068-9070	
8022	DS44-1000	PC 7918 (1ST)	
8023-8025	DS44-1000	PRR 9073, 9274, 9075	
8025 (2ND)	DS44-1000	PC 7935 (1ST)	
8026, 8027	DS44-1000	PRR 9076, 9077	
8028	DS44-1000	PC 7928 (1ST)	
8029, 8030	DS44-1000	PRR 9079, 9177	
8029 & 8030 (2ND)	DS44-1000	PC 7932 (1ST), 7930 (1ST)	
8031, 8032	DS44-1000	PRR 9431, 9432	
8031 & 8032 (2ND)	DS44-1000	PC 7938 (1ST), 7939 (1ST)	
8033, 8034, 8035, 8036	DS44-1000	PRR 9433, 9434, 9258, 9259	
8036 (2ND)	DS44-1000	PC 8041 (1ST)	
8037-8039	DS44-1000	PRR 9260, 5978, 5979	
8040-8043, 8044	DS44-1000	PRR 9180-9183, 9261	
8045, 8046	DS44-1000	PRR 9429, 9430	
8047, 8048	VO1000	NYC 9300, 9301	
8050, 8051-8053	DRS44-1000	PRR 9276, 5591-5593	
8062, 8063	LH 1200 RS	NYC 6210, 6211	
8067-8077, 8079-8083	RS12	NYC 6220-6230, 6232-6236	5
8084-8086	RS12	PRR 8975, 8110, 8776	
8087-8091	RS12	PRR 8107-8109, 8105-8106	
8093-8096,8098-8101	S12	NYC 9309-9312, 9314-9317	
8106-8108, 8110-8111	S12	NYC 9319-9321, 9326-9327	
8113, 8114, 8117, 8120	S12	PRR 8793, 8794, 8977, 8980	
8122, 8123, 8125, 8128-	S12	PRR 8982, 8983, 8985, 8988-	
8132, 8134-8136	S12	8992, 8104, 8100, 8101	
8138-8140, 8144-8147	S12	PRR 8778-8780, 8784-8787	
8149, 8151, 8152, 8153	S12	PRR 8789, 8791, 8792, 8753	
8154, 8156-8158, 8160-	S12	PRR 8754, 8756-8758, 8760-	
8164, 8165, 8166, 8167	S12	8764, 8102, 8976, 8103	
8168-8171, 8173, 8175	S12	PRR 8768-8771, 8773, 8775	
8176, 8177, 8179, 8180	S12	PRR 8766, 8767, 8765, 8750	
8182-8184, 8186, 8187	S12	PRR 8732-8734, 8736, 8737	
8189, 8190, 8192, 8193	S12	PRR 8739, 8740, 8742, 8743	
8195, 8197-8199	S12	PRR 8745, 8747-8749	
7800-7824 (2ND)	GP38	NEW 11/69	1
7825-7867 (2ND)	GP38	NEW 5, 6/70	1
7868-7939 (2ND)	GP38	NEW 1-3/71	1, 56
7940-8039 (2ND)	GP38-2	NEW 5-8/72	1, 57
8040-8153 (2ND)	GP38-2	NEW 1-3/73	1
8154-8162 (2ND)	GP38-2	NEW 10/73	1, 20
8207-8209	H10-44	NYC 9107-9109	
8211, 8212, 8215-8217	H10-44	PRR 5980, 5981, 5984-5986	
8218, 8219, 8223, 8224	H10-44	PRR 9184, 9185, 9189, 9190	
8227, 8229-8231, 8233-	H10-44	PRR 9193, 9195-9197, 9288-	
8235, 8237-8239, 8243	H10-44	9290, 9292-9294, 9299	
8244, 8248, 8250, 8252	H10-44	PRR 9080, 9084, 9086, 9089	
8254-8256, 8259, 8260	H10-44	PRR 9091-9093, 9096, 9097	
8263-8265	DS44-1000	PC (7952, 7956, 7959)(1ST)	
8266-8268	DS44-1000	PC (7960, 7966, 7968)(1ST)	
8269-8271	DS44-1000	PC (7969, 7973, 7978)(1ST)	
8272-8274	DS44-1000	PC (7980, 7981, 7996)(1ST)	
8275-8277	DS44-1000	PC (7997, 8003, 8007)(1ST)	
8278-8280	DS44-1000	PC (8010, 8014, 8018)(1ST)	
8281-8283	DS44-1000	PC (8019, 8022, 8023)(1ST)	
8284, 8285	DS44-1000	PC 8025 (2ND), 8026 (1ST)	
8286, 8287	DS44-1000	PC 8027 (1ST), 8028 (1ST)	
8288-8290	DS44-1000	PC 8029-8031 (ALL 2ND)	
8291, 8292	DS44-1000	PC 8032 (2ND), 8033 (1ST)	
8293, 8294	DS44-1000	PC 8034 (1ST), 8035 (1ST)	
8295, 8296	DS44-1000	PC ? , 8037 (1ST)	
8297	DS44-1000	PC ?	
8303, 8305, 8307, 8309-	H12-44	NYC 9114, 9116, 9118, 9120-	
8313, 8315, 8316, 8318	H12-44	9124, 9126, 9127, 9129	
8320, 8321, 8323-8326	H12-44	NYC 9131, 9132, 9134-9137	
8327, 8330, 8336	H12-44	PRR 8711, 8714, 8720	
8337, 8339-8342	H12-44	PRR 8721, 8723, 8708-8710	
8300-8302		DRS44-1000 PC 8050-8052 (1ST)	
8303 (2ND), 8304	RS12	PC 8053 (1ST), 8073 (1ST)	
8305 (2ND), 8306	RS12	PC 8082 (1ST), 8084 (1ST)	
8307 (2ND), 8308	S12	PC 8088 (1ST), 8094 (1ST)	
8309-8311 (ALL 2ND)	S12	PC (8096, 8098, 8099)(1ST)	
8312-8313 (ALL 2ND)	S12	PC 8100 & 8106 (ALL 1ST)	
8314, 8315 (2ND)	S12	PC 8107 & 8110 (ALL 1ST)	
8316 (2ND), 8317	S12	PC 8111 & 8113 (ALL 1ST)	
8318 (2ND), 8319	S12	PC 8114 & 8128 (ALL 1ST)	
8320-8321 (ALL 2ND)	S12	PC 8134 & 8138 (ALL 1ST)	
8322, 8323 (2ND)	S12	PC 8144 & 8149 (ALL 1ST)	
8324-8326 (ALL 2ND)	S12	PC (8152, 8154, 8157)(1ST)	
8327 (2ND), 8328	S12	PC 8158 & 8160 (ALL 1ST)	
8329, 8330 (2ND)	S12	PC 8162 (1ST), 8164	
8331-8334	S12	PC 8168, 8175, 8177, 8179	
8335, 8336 (2ND)	S12	PC 8180, 8182	

Locomotive Number	Model	Previous History	Notes	Locomotive Number	Model	Previous History	Notes
8337 (2ND), 8338	S12	PC 8183,8184		8803-8810	NW2	NYC 8803-8810	
8339-8342 (ALL 2ND)	S12	PC 8187, 8189, 8192, 8197		8836, 8837	SW7	NYC (CR&I) 8836, NYC 8837	
8343, 8344	S12	PC 8183, 8184		8838, 8839	SW7	NYC (CR&I) 8838, NYC 8839	
8350-8352	DS44-660	PC 7826-7828 (1ST)		8840, 8841	SW7	NYC (CR&I) 8840, 8841	
8353-8355	DS44- 660	PC (7832, 7834, 7835)(1ST)		8842-8850	SW7	IHB 8842-8850	
8356-8358	DS44-660	PC(7837,7839,7841))1st)		8851-8855	SW7	NYC 8851-8855	
8359-8361	DS44-660	PC (7843, 7845, 7847)(1ST)		8872-8874	SW7	IHB 8872-8874	
8362-8364	DS44-660	PC (7848, 7850, 7851)(1ST)		8880-8903	SW7	NYC 8880-8903	53
8365-8367	DS44-660	PC 7860-7862 (1ST)		8904-8906	SW7	NYC (P&E) 8904-8906	
8368-8370	DS44-660	PC (7865, 7867, 7869)(1ST)		8907	SW7	IHB 8715	
8371-8374	DS44-660	PC 7870-7873 (1ST)		8908-8910	SW7	NYC (P&E) 8908-8910	
8375-8377	DS44-660	PC (7877, 7880, 7881)(1ST)		8911-8921	SW9	NYC 8911-8921	
8378-8380	DS44-660	PC (7882, 7883, 7885)(1ST)		8922-8925, 8926	SW9	NYC 8922-8925, 8926 (2ND)	
8381-8383	DS44-750	PC (7886,7887,7892)(1st)		8927-8930, 8941-8951	`SW9	NYC 8927-8930, 8941-8951	
8384-8386	DS44-750	PC (7893, 7901, 7908)(1ST)		8962-9001	SW9	NYC 8962-9001	
8387, 8388	DS44-750	PC 7910 & 7912 (ALL 1ST)		9009-9034	SW1200	PRR 7909-7934	5
8398, 8399	LH 1200 RS	PC 8062 & 8063 (ALL 1ST)		9035-9037, 9038	SW7	PRR9365-9367, 9364	5
8400	SW1	NYC (CR&I) 574	58	9039-9041	SW7	PRR 9382, 9383, 9381	
8401, 8402	SW1	NYC 575, 576		9042-9044	SW9	PRR 8542-8544	
8403	SW1	NYC (CR&I) 577		9045-9049	SW7	PRR 9385, 9384, 9393-9395	
8403 (2ND)	SW1	PC 8415		9050-9058	SW1200	PRR 7900-7908	
8404, 8405, 8406	SW1	NYC 578-579, NYC (CR&I) 580		9059, 9060	SW9	PRR 8859, 8860	
8414, 8416-8419	SW1	NYC 581-588, 590-593	5, 53	9061-9067, 9068	SW7	PRR 8861-8867, 9368	
8420, 8421-8429	SW1	NYC (CR&I) 594, NYC 595-603		9069-9072, 9073-9075	SW7	PRR 9389-9392, 9373-9375	
8430	SW1	NYC (CR&I) 604		9075 (2ND)	NW2u	PC 8754	
8430 (2ND)	SW1	PC 8474		9076-9080	SW7	PRR 9376-9380	5
8431-8436, 8437	SW1	NYC 605-610, NYC (CR&I) 611		9081-9083, 9084-9089	SW7	PRR 9386-9388, 9358-9363	
8438-8443, 8444	SW1	NYC 612-617, NYC (CR&I) 618		9090-9093, 9094	SW7	PRR 9369-9372, 8868	
8445-8447, 8449-8452	SW1	NYC 619-621, 651-654		9095, 9096	SW9	PRR 8869, 8870	
8453, 8454-8458	SW1	NYC (CR&I) 655, NYC 656-660		9097, 9098	SW7	PRR 8871, 8872	
8459	SW1	NYC (CR&I) 661		9099-9103	NW2U	PC ? , 8654, 8696, 8673	63
8460-8472	SW1	NYC 662-666, 668-675		9104-9106	NW2U	PC ? , ?	63
8474-8497	SW1	NYC 676-695, 697-701		9107-9108	NW2u	PC ? , ?	63
8498, 8500	SW1	NYC (CR&I) 702, NYC 704		9109-9111	NW2u	PC ? , ? , ?	63
8501-8503, 8504	SW1	PRR 9201-9203, 9104		9113-9133	SW9	PRR 8513-8533	5
8505-8509, 8510	SW1	PRR 9205-9209, 5910		9133 (2ND)	NW2u	PC8704	63
8511	SW1	PRR 5911	59	9150-9152	NW2u	PC 9075, 8668, 8661	63
8512-8520, 8522-8528	SW1	PRR 9412-9420, 9422-9428	5	9153-9155	NW2u	PC 9133 (2ND), 8663, 8660	63
8530-8533, 8537-8543	SW1	PRR 9150-9153,9137-9143	5,53,60	9156-9158	NW2u	PC 8686, 8657, IHB 8733	63
8544-8553, 8554, 8556-	SW1	PRR 5944-5953, 9154, 9396-	5	9159-9163	NW2u	IHB 8735-8737, 8781, 8793	63
8571, 8575, 8576, 8578	SW1	9411, 9145, 9146, 9148		9164-9166	NW2u	IHB 8820, PC 8700, 8804	63
8579, 8580, 8587-8599	SW!	PRR 9149, 9200, 5987-5999	5	9167-9170	NW2u	PC 8702, 8764, 8655, 8810	63
8600-8605	SW8	NYC 9600-9605		9171-9174	NW2u	PC 8677, 8647, 8651, 8672	63
8605 (2ND)	SW8	DS1 15	61	9175-9177	NW2u	PC 8703, 8671, 8695	63
8606-8627	SW8	NYC 9606-9627		9178, 9179	NW2u	PC ? , ?	63
8628-8630	SW900	NYC (CUT) 9628-9630		9180-9199	SW1200	NH 640-659	
8631-8646	SW900	NYC 9631-9646		(9216-9221)	SW1500	NEW 6, 7/68	4
8647-8650, 8651-8654	NW2	PRR 9247-9250, 5921-5924		9223-9227	SW1500	NEW 6/70	1, 64
8655-8676, 8677, 8678	NW2	PRR 9155-9176, 5912, 5925	5	9300, 9301, 9303, 9305	S1	NYC 811, 812, 814, 816	
8683-8699	NW2	NYC 9500-9516	62	9307-9309, 9310, 9311	S1	NYC 819-821, 823, 824	65
8700-8704, 8750-8773	NW2	NYC 8700-8704, 9750-8773		9315, 9323, 9325, 9326	S1	NYC 829, 842, 845, 846	
8795-8802	NW2	IHB 8795-8802		9328,9334	S1	NYC 84 8, 857	

Locomotive Number	Model	Previous History	Notes
9335-9340, 9345-9347	S1	NYC 859-864, 870, 871, 873	65
9348-9350, 9352, 9354	S3	NYC 874-876, 878, 882	
9360, 9361, 9365, 9366	S3	NYC 889, 890, 895, 897	
9368, 9369, 9371-9373	S3	NYC 900, 901, 903-905	
9374, 9378, 9380	S3	NYC 907, 910-913, 915	
9382, 9383, 9384, 9385	S1	NYC 956, 818 822,825	
9389, 9392, 9393, 9394	S1	NYC 839, 852, 856, 858	
9395, 9396, 9398	S3	NYC 879, 880, 893	
9400-9402	S3	NYC 898, 906, 908	
9405, 9406, 9408	S1	NYC 951, 952, 954	
9411	HH660	NH 0924	66
9412-9414, 9415	S1	NH 0935-0937, 0940	
9416-9419, 9420	S1	NH 0944-0947, 0949	
9421-9424	S1	NH 0950, 0952, 0953, 0955	
9425-9435	S1	NH 0957-0963, 0965-0968	
9436	S1	NH 0970	
9437-9440, 9442-9446	S1	PRR 9237-9240, 9242-9246	
9447-9449	S1	NH 0972-0974	
9451, 9452, 9454-9456	S1	PRR 9101,9102, 5954-5956	
9457-9459	S1	NH 0975-0977	
9461-9463, 9465-9470	S1	PRR 5661-5663, 5665-5670	
9473-9477, 9479	S3	PRR 8873-8877, 8879	
9482-9485	S3	PRR 8882-8885	
9486-9493	S1	NH 0978-0983, 0985, 0986	
9494-9497	S1	NH 0988, 0989, 0991, 0992	
9498, 9499	S1	NH 0994, 0995	
9500-9509	SW1500	NEW 2/71	1
9510-9559	SW1500	NEW 2, 3/72	1
9560-9583	SW1500	NEW 9, 10/73	1
9600	S2	NYC 8500	
9601	S4	PC 9815	
9602-9604, 9605	S2	NYC 8502-8504, 8505 (2ND)	
9606-9609	S2	NYC 8506, 8508, 8509, 8511	
9611, 9613-9615	S2	NYC 8517, 8521, 8524, 8525	
9618, 9619, 9621, 9622	S2	NYC 8532, 8537, 8539, 8540	
9623, 9624, 9626, 9627	S2	NYC 8542, 8543, 8545, 8549	
9628,9629, 9631-9641	S2	NYC 8518, 8551, 8556-8566	
9643-9658, 9660, 9661	S2	NYC 8568-8584, 8586, 8588	
9663-9669, 9671	S4	NYC 8590-8596, 8599	
9673-9692	S4	NYC 8601-8618	
9693, 9694-9703	S4	8621, 8622, 8624-8632	
9704, 9705	S2	NYC 851 & 869 (ALL 2ND)	
9706-9708, 9710	S2	NYC 8507, 8510, 8512, 8515	
9712, 9713, 9716-9718	S2	NYC 8518, 8519, 8526-8528	
9719, 9720, 9722	S2	NYC 8531, 8533, 8534	
9723-9725, 9727	S2	NYC 8536, 8553, 8554, 8581	
9729, 9730	S4	NYC 8598, 8623	

Locomotive Number	Model	Previous History	Notes
9731, 9732	S2	NYC 8541, 8548	
9733-9737, 9739-9741	S4	NYC 8633-8637, 8639-8641	
9743-9746, 9748, 9751-9753, 9756-9759, 9761	S4	NYC 8643-8646, 8648, 8651-8653, 8656-8659, 8661	
9763, 9765	S4	NYC 8663, 8665	
9768, 9769, 9770	S4	PRR 8498, 8499, 8490	
9771-9777	S4	PRR 8491-8497	
9778-9784, 9785	S2	PRR 9278-9284, 5655	5
9786, 9787	S2	PRR 9286, 9287	
9788-9796, 9798	S4	PRR 8888-8896, 8898	
9799-9801	S4	PRR 8899, 8900, 8901	
9802	S2	PRR 5660	
9803	S4	PRR 8886	
9804, 9805-9809	S2	PRR 9204, 9105-9109	5
9810, 9812-9814	S2	PRR 5650, 5652-5654	5
9815	S4	PRR 8487	
9816	S2	PRR 5646	
9817	S4	PRR 8887	
9818-9821	S2	PRR 5648, 5649, 5930, 5931	
9822, 9823	S4	PRR 8488, 8489	5
9824, 9825, 9826-9828	S2	PRR 5644, 5645, 5926-5928	5
9830-9834	S4	PRR 8430-8434	
9836-9839, 9841, 9842	S2	PRR 5656-5659, 5641, 5642	
9844-9849	T6	PRR 8424-8429	
9850-9853	S2	NH 0600, 0601, 0603, 0606	
9854-9857	S2	NH 0608-0610, 0615	
9858-9860	S2	NH 0616, 0618, 0621	
9900-9913	RS1	NYC 8100-8113	
9914-9917	RS1	PRR 8485, 8486, 5906, 8857	
9918-9927	RS1	PRR 8858, 5619-5627	5
9929-9940	RS1	PRR 5629-5640	5, 65
9941-9946	RS1	NH 0662-0665, 0667, 0671	
9948	SLUG	PC 6803 (2ND)	67
9949	AEH-12	PC 6811	67
9949A, 9949B	AEH-12	PC 9949, 9948	67
9950-9953	RS3m	PC 5477, 5230, 5240, 5242	68
9954-9957	RS3m	PC 5227, 5526, 5470, 5342	
9958-9961	RS3m	PC 5360, 5400, 5589, 5228	
9962-9963	RS3m	PC 5487, 5567	
9963 (2ND), 9964	RS3m	PC 5257, 5243	
9965-9968	RS3m	PC 5241, 5318, 5555, 5333	
9969-9972	RS3m	PC 5288, 5403, 5238, 5464	
9973-9976	RS3m	PC 5532, 5328, 5578, 5508	
9977-9980	RS3m	PC 5290, 5405, 5544, 5590	
9981-9984	RS3m	PC 5585, 5364, 5596, 5260	
9999	GE 44 T	PRR 9353	

ROSTER NOTES

1. THE FOLLOWING 1038 LOCOMOTIVES WERE PURCHASED NEW BY THE PENN CENTRAL:

6540-6559 [B/N 36670-36689, B/D 2-4-68]
6330-6344 [B/N 3499-01 - 3499-15, B/D 2--/68]
6235-6239 [O/N 7125, B/N 34277-34281, B/D 8-68]
6560-6563 [B/N 36864-36867, B/D 8-68]
3105-3169 [O/N 7127, B/N 34546-34610, B/D 8-68]
3170-3259 [O/N 7145, B/N 34611-34700, B/D 10-12-68]
2890-2955 [B/N 36868-36933, B/D 9-12-68]
7675-7814 [O/N 7191, B/N 35304-35428, B/D 6-11-69]
7815-7824 [O/N 7202, B/N 35444-35453, B/D 11-69]
6925-6959 [O/N 7264, B/N 36406-36438, B/D 4-70]
7825-7867 [O/N 7265, B/N 36441-36483, B/D 5, 670]
2956-2970 [B/N 37396-37410, B/D 5, 6-70]
9223-9227 [O/N 7262, B/N 36381-36385, B/D 6-70]
2010-2014 [O/N 7281, B/N 36801-36805, B/D 7, 8-70]
6700-6711 [B/N 37540-37551, B/D 10-70]
6712-6718 [B/N 37552-37558, B/D 11-70]
6240-6270 [O/N 7290, B/N 36896-36926, B/D 12-70/1-70]
6271-6284 [O/N 7290, B/N 36997-37010, B/D 1, 2-71]
7868-7903 [O/N 7291, B/N 36927-36962, B/D 1, 2-71]
7904-7907 [O/N 7299, B/N 36993-36996, B/D 3-71]
7908-7939 [O/N 7291, B/N 36963-36992, 37011-
   37012, B/D 2, 3-71]
9500-9509 [O/N 7292, B/N 37058-37067, B/D 2-71]
9510-9559 [B/N 7355-1 - 7355-50, B/D 2, 3-72]
7940-8039 [B/N 7354-1 - 7354-100, B/D 5-8-72]
2700-2749 [B/N 38506-38555, B/D 8-10-72]
8040-8153 [B/N 72627-1 - 72627-114, B/D 1-3-73]
2750-2776 [B/N 39305-39331, B/D 8-10-73]
9560-9583 [B/N 73622-1 - 73622-24, B/D 9, 10-73]
8154-8162 [B/N 73608-1 - 73608-9, B/D 10-73]

2. PC 3260-3274 WERE ORIGINALLY EMD 11-20, 22-26[B/N 35044-35053, 35055-35059, B/D 4, 5-69]. THEY WERE BUILT BY EMD AS LOANERS WHILE SOME RAILROADS RETURNED THEIR GP35'S & GP40'S BACK TO EMD FOR FRAME AND CRANKSHAFT PROBLEM REPAIRS. PC BOUGHT THEM 2/70.

3. 2809-2811 WERE LEASED FROM P&LE FROM 1969 TO 1971 TO RELIEVE A MOTIVE POWER SHORTAGE AND RECEIVED PC PAINT AND LOGOS.

4. 9216-9221 [O/N 7111, B/N 34030-34035, B/D 6, 7/68] WERE ORIGINALLY ORDERED BY PC, PAINTED PC AND THEN TURNED OVER TO SUBSIDIARY IHB AND REPAINTED IHB COLORS. THEY NEVER WORKED FOR PC.

5. THE FOLLOWING UNITS ARE KNOWN TO HAVE BEEN PAINTED WITH RED P LOGOS DURING APRIL TO JUNE 1968:

1350, 1646, 1665, 1707, 1709, 1713, 1734, 1760, 1773, 1792, 1796, 1839, 2110, 2189, 2198, 2201, 2203-2205, 2209, 2211, 2213, 2220, 2226, 2232, 2234-2238, 2246, 2252, 2254, 2255, 2263, 2267, 2282, 2291, 2294, 2317, 2329, 2337, 2375, 2381-2383, 2385-2387, 2389, 2395, 2398, 2404, 2405, 2422, 2647, 2650, 3001, 3802, 4247, 4249, 4254, 4292, 4312, 4347, 4367, 4370, 4422, 4440, 4442, 4443, 4862, 4902, 4906, 4915, 4932, 5461, 6018, 6020, 6023, 6035, 6070, 6093, 6095, 6122, 6125, 6133, 6139, 6162, 6304, 6312, 6557, 6809, 6812, 6814, 6861, 6865, 6867, 6868, 6870, 6871, 6912, 7029, 7045, 7075, 7077, 7080, 7097, 7106, 7126, 7142, 7231, 7232, 7243, 7245, 7265, 7415, 7444, 7502, 7650, 8085, 8413, 8523, 8539, 8558, 8587, 8596, 8674, 9020, 9021, 9023, 9025, 9034, 9035, 9077, 9080, 9117, 9779, 9806, 9812, 9822, 9825, 9921, 9924, 9925, 9933

6. THE FOLLOWING UNITS ARE KNOWN TO HAVE BEEN PAINTED WITH ORANGE C LOGOS: 3170-3186 (10/68), 5585 (LAST WEEK OF 4/69)

7. ASSIGNED TO THE MERCHANTS DESPATCH SHOPS IN E. ROCHESTER, N.Y., 15 WORE A UNIQUE PAINT SCHEME DESIGNED BY SHOP FORCES. IT WAS PAINTED BRUNSWICK GREEN WITH A LARGE CENTURY GREEN BAND ACROSS ITS FLANK AND WHITE TRIM AND FRAME STRIPE. IT WAS LETTERED DESPATCH SHOPS, INC. WITH SLANT LETTERING.

8. ON 2/28/70 PC BOUGHT 10 D&RGW F UNITS FOR TRADE-IN ON EMD ORDER 7202 (GP38 7815-7824). F7A 5721 & 5754 AND F7B 5712 & 5733 WERE MECHANICALLY SOUND AND KEPT FOR SERVICE. THE OTHER UNITS, F7A 5641 & 5691 AND F7B 5642, 5662, 5663 & 5673 WERE SENT DEAD TO EMD.

9. THE LAST ALCO FA'S (1302, 1330, 1331, 1333) WERE RETIRED 6/23/71.

10. PRR 1408 WAS THE ONLY PRR F3A UNIT WITH CHICKEN-WIRE GRILLS TO SEE SERVICE PAST THE PC MERGER.

11. 1450, 1482, 1501, 1905 & 3547 WERE THE ONLY PRR FREIGHT F UNITS TO BE PAINTED IN FULL PC PAINT.

12. THE EX D&RGW UNITS DID NOT RECEIVE FULL PC PAINT UNTIL LATE 8/72.

13. 2010-2014 WERE DELIVERED TO BLUE ISLAND YD. 11/14/70 PAINTED PRSL BUT PRSL COULDN'T GET FINANCING TO PAY FOR THEM. THEY WERE THEN SOLD TO PC AND BY 11/21/70 WORE PC DRESS.

14. THESE WERE THE LAST NEW UNITS PURCHASED BY THE NEW YORK CENTRAL.

15. PC 2399, NEE NYC 6155 WAS EMD'S DISPLAY ENGINE AT THE 1964-65 N.Y. WORLD'S FAIR.

16. 2415 WAS BUILT WITH ELECTRICAL COMPONENTS FROM ALCO DL640 DEMONSTRATOR 640-1.

17. THE FOLLOWING WERE CONTROL & SLAVE UNITS: 2555/2535, 6300/6301, & 6100/6101.

18. 2600, 2611 & 2623 WERE UPGRADED TO 2800HP.

19. NH 2510-2525 WERE THE LAST NEW UNITS BOUGHT BY THE NEW HAVEN.

20. PC 2750-2776 AND 8154-8162 CAME EQUIPPED WITH DUAL CONTROLS AND WERE SET UP TO RUN LONG END FORWARD.

21. NYC 2858 & 2859 WERE GE'S FIRST PRODUCTION UNITS FOR THE U33B MODEL.

22. NYC 2889 WAS GE'S 1,000TH DIESEL ROAD UNIT BUILT.

23. 2956-2970 WERE ORIGINALLY ORDERED BY ROCK ISLAND (TO HAVE BEEN R.I. 4510-4524) BUT WERE CANCELLED DURING THE 1-2/70 GE STRIKE DUE TO LACK OF FINANCING.

24. NYC 3036 WAS EMD'S FIRST PRODUCTION UNIT WITH THE NEW 645 ENGINE (THE FIRST GP40 OF ORDER 7851, B/N 30973, B/D 11/65).

25. NYC 4003 & 4020 WERE REBUILT AND UPGRADED BY EMD TO 2250 HP FOLLOWING WRECKS.

26. 4273, 4284 & 4293 RECEIVED FULL REPAINTING IN TUSCAN DURING 11/70 AND CARRIED PC LOGOS.

27. 4269 CARRIED A SMALL AMTRAK LOGO ON ONE SIDE 5/71 LONG BEFORE BEING PURCHASED BY AMTRAK IN 1972.

28. 4300 WAS THE ONLY PRR EMD E UNIT THAT HAD AN OSCILLATING HEADLIGHT AS WELL AS A NOSE HEADLIGHT.

29. 4316 WORE AMTRAK'S FIRST PAINT SCHEME ON 5/1/71.

30. IN OCT. 1973 THESE EX NYC UNITS , BEING SURPLUS, WERE FITTED WITH CAB SIGNALS, RENUMBERED, AND SENT TO WORK OUT THEIR LIVES ON THE NY & LB.

31. GG1'S 4901 & 4903 WERE USED TO PULL THE R. F. KENNEDY FUNERAL TRAIN WITH 4932 (RED P) AND 3 CARS AS A PILOT TRAIN AND 4900 & 4910 AS REAR PROTECT UNITS.

32. 4902 WORE THE AMERICAN RAILROADS PAINT SCHEME (DESIGNED BY NOTED RR PAINTER AND PHOTOGRAPHER ROBERT LORENZ) FROM EARLY1969 UNTIL APRIL 1970.

33. THE FOLLOWING FL9'S RECEIVED PC BLACK PAINT: FULL SCHEME- 5003, 5010 (1ST UNIT), 5011, 5013-5015, 5024, 5026, 5027, 5050; E8 SIZE LOGO ONLY-5020; LOGO ONLY- 5000, 5005, 5007, 5018, 5019, 5022, 5032, 5038, 5043; NO. ONLY- 5040.

34. THE FOLLOWING FL9'S KEPT NEW HAVEN PAINT UNTIL CONRAIL: 5001, 5006, 5008, 5009, 5023, 5025, 5029, 5030, 5035, 5048, 5051.

35. THE FOLLOWING FL9'S RECEIVED MTA BLUE & YELLOW: 5000, 5002-05, 5007, 5010, 5012-22, 5024, 5026-28, 5031, 5033, 5034, 5036-39, 5041-47, 5049, 5050, 5052. 5014 & 5050 WERE THE FIRST MTA FL9'S; PAINTED 7/28/70.

36. 5158 WAS THE ONLY UNIT PAINTED PC THAT HAD SLANT NUMBERS.

37. IN 1972 PC REBUILT RS3 5477 USING COMPONENTS AND THE 12-657 ENGINE FROM A RETIRED E8. IT WAS RELEASED FROM THE ALTOONA SHOPS 4/7/72 WITH THE TYPICAL FRONT RS SHORT HOOD COMPLETELY MISSING.

38. RS3 5230 UNDERWENT THE SAME REBUILD AT ALTOONA AS 5477 HAD AND WAS RELEASED FOR SERVICE WITH A CHOP-NOSE ON 7/16/73.

39. FOLLOWING THE ALTOONA SUCCESSES (5477 & 5230), 5240 BECAME THE FIRST OFFICIAL "DEWITT GEEP". REBUILT DURING 8/73 AT THE DEWITT, N.Y. SHOPS, IT ALSO RECEIVED A 12-657 EMD ENGINE AND COMPONENTS FROM A RETIRED E8.

40. 5242 BECAME THE 2ND "DEWITT GEEP", OUT SHOPPED FROM DEWITT ON 9/17/73.

41. DURING 4/71 THE LEHIGH VALLEY TRADED TO PC TWO OUT-OF-SERVICE RS2'S FOR TWO IN-SERVICE PC RS3'S. PC 5401 BECAME LV 212 (2ND) AND PC 5461 BECAME LV 210 (2ND). THE LV UNITS WERE RENUMBERED INTO PC AND SENT TO GE AS TRADE-INS.

42. THE 5500 SERIES RS3'S, 5900 SERIES GP7'S, 7500 SERIES GP9'S, AND GP9 7300-7303 WERE ALL STEAM GENERATOR EQUIPPED FOR PASSENGER SERVICE.

43. THE LEHIGH VALLEY BOUGHT HIGH-HOOD RS3 5569 ON 5/3/70 TO SUPPLEMENT ITS AILING RS2 & 3 FLEET AND TRADED TO PC CANNIBILIZED RS2 211. 5569 BECAME LV 211 (2ND) AND WAS PAINTED LV COLORS BY 7/22/70. THE LV RS2 WAS RENUMBERED PC 5569 (2ND) AND USED AS TRADE-IN MATERIAL.

44. IRONICALLY, ON FEB. 1, 1968 (MERGER DAY) AT COLLINWOOD SHOPS, GP7 5609 RECEIVED THE LAST OFFICIAL PAINTING IN THE NYC SCHEME.

45. 5818-5827, EX NYC (NEE C&O 5720-5729 ACQUIRED 1/56) AND 7429-7440 EX NYC WERE CANADIAN GMDL BUILT AND USED ON THE CANADA SOUTHERN DIVISION.

46. DURING 11/70 IN CHICAGO PC LET A NUMBER OF HANDICAPPED CHILDREN BEGIN PAINTING EX NYC GP7 5916 WHITE. SHOP FORCES LATER COMPLETED THE JOB WITH BLACK FRAME AND RUNNING GEAR, WHITE CARBODY, AND THE SLOGAN "CRUSADE OF MERCY" IN RED ON THE LONG HOOD. "50,000.00" IN RED LETTERING (A LOCAL PC GOAL) WAS PLACED ON THE CAB AS A PUBLICITY VENTURE. IT CARRIED NO PC LOGOS OR NAME FOR IDENTIFICATION.

47. 6072 WAS THE FIRST UNIT TO RECEIVE THE PENN CENTRAL SCHEME. IT WAS DISPLAYED IN PHILADELPHIA, PA. ON MERGER DAY FOR THE PUBLIC TO SEE.

48. SD45 6200 - 6234 WERE THE LAST NEW UNITS PURCHASED BY THE PRR.

49. 6207 WAS THE LAST UNIT PAINTED PRR.

50. IN 2/69 6500, 6501, & 6502 WERE MODIFIED WITH CREEPER CONTROL SO THEY COULD TRAVEL 1/4MPH WHEN LOADING UNIT PP&L COAL TRAINS AT TUNNELTON, PA. 6200, 6201, & 6202 WERE SIMILARLY MODIFIED LATER.

51. PC 6540 WAS THE FIRST U33C BUILT.

52. 6803 AND 6804 SWAPPED NUMBERS EARLY JUNE 1974.

53. THE FOLLOWING UNITS RECEIVED A WHITE FRAME STRIPE AS PART OF A FULL PC RE PAINTING:

6900, 6914, 8414, 8544, 8865, 8883, 8946, 8970, 9185, 9476 (THIS LAST UNIT ALSO HAD SILVER TRUCKS).

54. THE SD38'S WERE THE FIRST UNITS TO CARRY PC'S NEW STYLE OF NUMBERS.

55. GP38'S 7675-7737 ORIGINALLY CAME WITH CONVENTIONAL OIL-BATH AIR FILTERS; BEGINNING WITH 7738 THEY CAME WITH THE NEW IMPROVED PAPER AIR FILTERS.

56. 7934 & 7935 WERE ORDERED BY LEHIGH VALLEY BUT WERE SOLD AS PART OF A PC ORDER WHEN LV DEVELOPED FINANCIAL PROBLEMS.

57. 30 PLUS GP38-2'S, BEGINNING WITH 7940, WERE DELIVERED WITH WHITE NUMBER BOARDS (ALA NYC U30B'S), WHICH WERE STANDARD FOR EMD UNITS. THEY WERE CHANGED BY PC TO THEIR STANDARD BLACK BOARDS (AN OPTION WITH EMD) A FEW MONTHS LATER.

58. 8400 (EX-NYC 574, BLT. 2/39) BECAME PC'S OLDEST UNIT AFTER 8511 (EX-PRR 5911, BLT 6/37) WAS RETIRED IN 1968. 8400 LASTED WELL INTO CONRAIL.

59. 8511, EX PRR 5911, WAS PRR'S FIRST DIESEL SWITCHER.

60. 8544 WAS REPAINTED DURING 12/71 WITH A WHITE FRAME STRIPE, SILVER TRUCKS AND RECEIVED THE TITLE G. H. BASHANT ON THE CAB.

61. DSI 15 WAS RENUMBERED PC 8605 AROUND IN EARLY 1970.

62. NYC NW2 9500-9516 ARE EX NYO&W 114, 116-131 BOUGHT IN 1957.

63. IN EARLY 1969 PC BEGAN A CAPITAL OVER HAUL PROGRAM TO REBUILD ITS AGING SWITCHER FLEET. NW2'S, SW7'S & SW9'S FROM BOTH PC AND IHB WERE REBUILT AND UPGRADED TO 1200HP, AND RENUMBERED INTO THE PC SYSTEM.

64. 9223-9227 WERE DELIVERED 11/14/70 AT BLUE ISLAND YD. PAINTED IHB BUT IHB HAD A SIMILAR FINANCIAL SITUATION TO THE PRSL 2000 SERIES GP38'S. THE UNITS WERE RETURNED TO EMD, SOLD TO THE PC, AND BY 11/28/70 WERE IN PC PAINT.

65. 9337 & 9931 CARRIED EXPERIMENTAL RED REFLECTIVE STRIPES ON THEIR NOSES WHILE 9311 HAD TWO RED REFLECTIVE STRIPES ON THE CAB END BELOW THE WINDOWS.

66. 9411 WAS RETIRED 3/71.

67. LATE 1/75 PC BUILT AN EXPERIMENTAL HUMP SLUG SET AT DEWITT, N. Y. 6811 WAS REENGINED WITH AN EMD 12-657 PRIME MOVER AND 6803 (2ND) HAD ITS ENGINE REMOVED AND BALLASTED FOR EXTRA TRACTION. THE RADIATOR AREA WAS REMOVED ON 6803 AND REPLACED WITH THE SHORT HOOD OF 9901. INITIALLY NUMBERED 9948 (THE HUMP CONVERSION SLUG) & 9949 (THE MASTER), THEY LATER WERE BOTH NUMBERED 9949. A SECOND SLUG SET WAS PLANNED USING PC 6815 & 6801, BOTH TO BE NUMBERED 9948, BUT IT WAS DROPPED WITH THE ADVENT OF CONRAIL.

68. IN DEC. 1973 THE REBUILT RS3'S WERE RENUMBERED INTO THE 9950 SERIES AND IN JAN. 1974 THE 'DEWITT GEEP' REBUILD PROGRAM BEGAN IN EARNEST, LASTING INTO CONRAIL. PC 9984 WAS THE LAST PC ERA RS3m REBUILD.

GENERAL NOTES

A. ON MERGER DAY, FEB. 1, 1968, 1,802 LOCOMO-TIVES OF THE NEW YORK CENTRAL SYSTEM AND 2,277 LOCOMOTIVES OF THE PENNSYLVA-NIA RAILROAD BECAME THE ROSTER OF THE PENN CENTRAL.

B. ON JAN. 1, 1969, 313 LOCOMOTIVES FROM THE NEW HAVEN RAILROAD JOINED THE PENN CENTRAL ROSTER.

C. THE FOLLOWING E UNITS WERE BOUGHT BY AMTRAK IN 1972 AND RENUMBERED AS FOL-LOWS:

AMTRAK 255-324 WERE EX-PC 4020, 4036, 4038, 4040, 4041, 4043-4045, 4047-4049, 4051-4061, 4250, 4252, 4269, 4271, 4273-4284, 4286-4304, 4306-4317, 4319.

D. THE FOLLOWING GG1'S WERE BOUGHT BY AM-TRAK IN 1972 AND RENUMBERED AS FOLLOWS:

AMTRAK 902, 908, 931 (ALL 1ST) WERE EX-PC 4902, 4908, 4931 (RENUMBERED IN 1972). THEN

AMTRAK 900-929 WERE EX-PC 4892, 4897, 4899, 4900-4903, 4906-4908, 4910-4914, 4916, 4918-4920, 4924-4926, 4928, 4929, 4931-4934, 4937, 4938 (RENUMBERED AROUND 3/15/73).

E. 4930-4938 (2ND), 4939 WERE RENUMBERED 7/73 FOLLOWING AMTRAK'S RENUMBERING OF THEIR GG1'S INTO A SOLID BLOCK (900-929) SO NO TWO GG1'S WOULD HAVE THE SAME LAST 3 DIGITS. THESE 10 UNITS WERE SUBSQUENTLY LONG-TERM LEASED TO AMTRAK.

F. ON APRIL 1, 1976, WHEN THE CONSOLDATED RAIL CORPORATION BECAME A REALITY, THE PENN CENTRAL CONTRIBUTED 3,927 LOCOMO-TIVES TO CONRAIL'S START-UP ROSTER. OF THOSE LOCOMOTIVES, 1,208 CAME FROM THE NEW YORK CENTRAL, 1,449 CAME FROM THE PENNSYLVANIA, 213 CAME FROM THE NEW HAVEN, 1,038 WERE BOUGHT NEW, AND 19 WERE MISCELLANEOUS ACQUISITIONS.

G. ALSO ON APRIL 1, 1976, 81 LOCOMOTIVES FROM THE PENN CENTRAL WERE SOLD TO AMTRAK, OF WHICH 34 CAME FROM THE NEW YORK CENTRAL, 29 CAME FROM THE PENNSYL VANIA, AND 18 CAME FROM THE NEW HAVEN.

Odds
&
Ends

Pictured on these two pages are a few of the creatures which don't quite fit on the Penn Central Locomotive roster for various reasons.

(Left, top & center) At first glance there appears nothing unusual about PC 9072. It was originally built in March 1950 as PRR 9392, a stock EMD SW7. In the top and the center photos, however, taken in August 1976 in Altoona, the unit displays a bulge on the roof in front of the exhaust stacks which resulted from a Conrail implantation of a surplus EMD V12 and roof fan assembly from a retired E8. Flush with Federal monies to rebuild the locomotive fleet, the 9072 was an early product of Altoona Works, but lacking a Conrail paint scheme from April to June 1976, the "SW7m" was cleaned up and released in its PC paint for the time being. Later in June 1976, Conrail releasing such rebuilds in its new blue scheme.

(Bottom) PC 80041 was one of two early Penn Central attempts to provide a mid-train remote control power unit for the ballast cleaning train. Built from a SW1 the little 80041 is more properly designated as a power generator car. Shown at Columbia, Pa., July 1969.

R.J. Yanosey

Herbert H. Harwood, RJY Collection

In the cities of Baltimore and Jersey City, N.J., the PRR and then Penn Central maintained a few rubber-tired "switchers" for use on streets with tight curves and auto traffic. Penn Central #3, a Grove tractor fitted with knuckles on both ends, switches 4 freight cars in Baltimore, February 1975.

Herbert H. Harwood, RJY Collection

In 1968, Penn Central was faced with scrapping GG1 4846, but decided to salvage something by cutting the unit in half and creating this "snow blower" shown at Wilmington, De., July 1980. Since the GG1 has often been cited as being "two units in one," the halving came naturally enough using the transformer end and applying sheet metal over the resulting opening. The "G 1/2" (?) was kept captive at Wilmington and never numbered.

Herbert H. Harwood

R.J. Yanosey

In 1964, the Pennsylvania Railroad leased 6 DL701's to subsidiary Lehigh Valley. Prior to their send off, Altoona upgraded the units to 2000 hp, and the diesels went to work on the Valley in PRR dress with 8600 series numbers. In 1966, the PRR-NYC renumbering caused the Alcos to be renumbered 7640-7644 and 7648, and they were soon painted into a Tuscan red with yellow stripe (ala PRR) LV paint scheme. The lease continued right through PC and into CR although these PC diesels never saw their true parent's black paint. LV 7648 is shown at Bethlehem, Pa. in one of Valley's several paint schemes, April 1975.

One Day On The Road
Thursday
February 20, 1975

The day Thursday, February 20, 1975, has no special significance in Penn Central train operations history. In fact, it was selected simply because it was a typical, middle of the week, workday on the railroad. By the latter part of PC's lifetime, the dust had settled quite a bit and many of the exotic paint schemes and power combinations were gone. Through freights were handled by second generation GM or GE hood units and only infrequently would an Alco appear. The railroad was doing what was required of it to survive: moving freight, and doing it with the most dependable, least expensive power possible.

Throughout this book, there are many photographs taken on the legendary ex PRR "Middle Division." The dispatcher sheet, technically the "PENN CENTRAL, CENTRAL REGION, ALLEGHENY DIVISION, Dispatcher's Record of Movement of Trains" on the opposite page, is one from that Division. The Main Line portion that we have excerpted on pages 248 and 249 extends from "Banks" just west of Harrisburg to "Antis" just east of Altoona, Pa; a very busy portion of the PC that funneled the train movement from many branches and mains at their extremities. While the trains shown passed several other interlock-

ings, we will only identify the entrance and exit times at Banks and Antis. A complete list of the interlockings is as follows: (going west) Banks, View, Port, Mifflin, Wall, Lewis, Jacks, Hunt, Deer, Pete, Spruce, Gray, and Antis. For our purposes, several Burro Crane, High Rail Vehicle, Work train, and "light return movements" have been omitted. The unusual occurrences have been copied verbatim from the sheet.

Take a good look at February 20, 1975, just another day on the bankrupt Penn Central.

It was cloudy and not too cold (32-44 degrees). By 1975 locomotives, cars, tracks and structures were not receiving anything like the attention they required, yet the people of Penn Central carried on throughout these hard times. They were truly the "glue" that held the system together. Despite what some thought of this Company, and despite its bare coffers, the record shows that Penn Central moved some of the heaviest traffic in the world. February 20, 1975 was business as usual on PC; truly a vital link in the American transportation system.

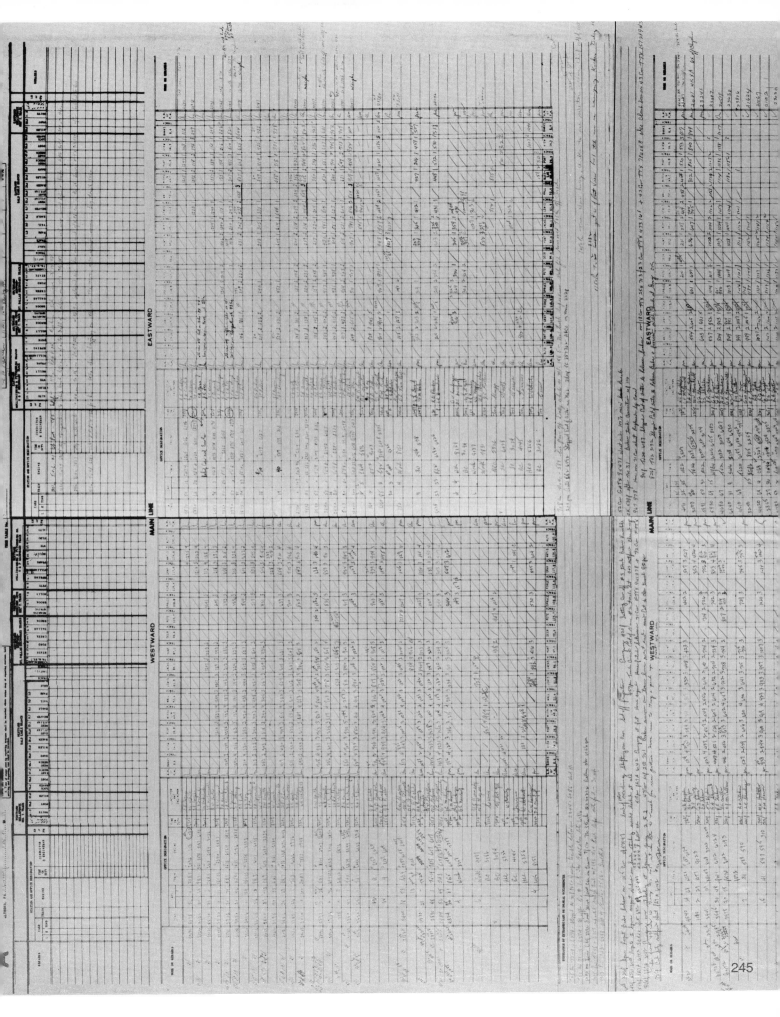

WESTWARD

TRAIN	ENGINE	CARS	TONS	"BANKS"	"ANTIS"	REMARKS
ZSR 7	6032-6131-6060	86/0	8098	---	1235	6060 not loading
PR 1	3121-2298-8127-6152	30/65	4726	---	1223	
ZSR 5	6213-6084-6022	85/0	8870	---	128	
XEC 53	2340-2857	0/111	3330	---	236	
RR 1	2275-2524-7874	30/74	3912	1229	318	42 hoppers
NJC 1	7825-3196-2838	30/46	4450	1246	332	
XEC 55	6258-2533	0/124	3416	310	622	
PR 3	6038-6101	36/13	2665	313	545	
PR 9	6113-6030-2334	39/12	2800	253	518	
SA 1	8121-6334	40/33	3795	325(Gray)	413	
PR 7	7872-2368-2196-8042	34/29	3886	419	710	
TV 3	6166-7976	26/1	1785	511	706	
JMA 1	7883-7948	0/100	3010	542	903	All covered hoppers
EH 1	8101-2907-6007	17/46	2597	708	146	6007 DIT
UFY 623	8123-3011-7850	0/96	2976	556	911	All PPLX (PP&L) hoppers
LH 13	5876	0/7	175	538 (Lewis)	658(Hunt)	
TV 11	6274-2344-6086	47/1	2350	651	947	
TV 1	6044-6223-2918	65/1	4620	822	1126	
# 11	6153-6262	12/0	---	716	954	
# 9	6127-6104	32/0	---	929	1158	
CB 9	2292-3098-6307	18/73	3420	813	129	6307 DIT
Yard	9125	0/13	---	854(Jacks)	906(Hunt)	
TV 25	6157-2939	A.M. 21/0	1470	1043	101	No push
TV 19	7827-6017-6117	P.M. 48/1	2890	1215	250	
JH 3	6198-6238-2566	36/49	3484	1213	317	6238 dead
PG 5	6048-8004-7719	35/81	4374	116	612	
Work	8151	4/0	---	149(Spruce)	157(Forge)	
Work	9137	6/0	---	737(Lewis)	1102(Jacks)	# 1 track A.M.
NJC 1	6150-3074	34/68	4540	154	527	
AT 1	9023	2/29	1010	353(Gray)	426	
XEC 57	8108-3202-2600	0/111	2941	427	910	
PW 1	6112-6124	30/48	3545	447	919	
PR 7A	6142-2193	30/78	3978	446	1044	#1 tunnel Spruce
# 31	Amtrak 588-590	7	---	527	755	
# 41	Amtrak 597-595-310	15	---	838	1042	
PR 1	6250-6121-6278	17/89	3475	904	1126	
CB 9	3180-6330	24/60	3598	952	---	
RR 1	6026-6192	36/29	3068	1122	---	

Extraordinary or Unusual Occurrences

7:05am TV 11 - 6274 - stopped at MP121 - Jumper trouble between 2344-6086 OK

7:50am TV 11 - 6274 - Mifflin - Excitation Lite 6086

10:40am Lewis CB 9 2292 Fired Servo first car in train #3 trk EL 20212 Roller Ok 1056am

12:15pm TV 25 - 6157 reported rough track MP 196 #2 track. Supvr. notified - 30 mph

12:13pm JH 3 - 6238 - Out of Enola - 2566 - isolated

3:26pm PG 5 - 6048 Spruce reports bands broken on 105th car UP 57947, load of farm machinery shifting on car.

Emergency 4:20pm setting car off #3 track, broken knuckle 52nd car GATX 95471 west end 100% new break

4:42pm NJC 1 6150 reports to Spruce magnet valve on sand sticking needs looking at

5:12pm PR 7A 6142 Servo PORT 69th car SP 225437 Roller OK

5:18 pm PR 7A 6142 Emergency at PORT home signal. Hoses parted between 71st car FTTX 941978 and 72nd car FTTX 967978. Hose on 71st car short, Replaced by crew.

8:16pm PR 7A Emergency over interlocking at Spruce going 2 to 2. 47th car MP 250761 broken union on train line west end. Moved east to clear tunnel 9:50pm. Take front 47 cars to Gray. Set out, lite to tunnel for rear portion. Move rear to Gray & pick up front 46 cars.

9:25pm Supvr notified about PR 7A and shop car.

EASTWARD

TRAIN	ENGINE	CARS	TONS	"ANTIS"	"BANKS"	REMARKS
CNY 4	6265-6166-6146	54/12	4070	---	112	
OE 8A	6020-6011-2343	62/32	5830	---	249	Recrewed Cove
CG 8	2292-3098-8125-2675	98/3	6555	---	208	
PF 6	6262-6153	57/26	4260	---	226	
TV 2	2934-2951-2959-2913	57/0	3990	---	520	Recrewed Thompsontown
PE 10a	7827-6017-6117	97/29	7875	106	644	
8/ 10	6179-6127	32/0	----	215	432	
# 40	Amtrak 589-599-313	14	----	528	738	
XMG 46	6314-6315	0/109	2750	108	513	
UE 622	2325-3002-2600-6250	85/0	9532	123	823	Alternator NW properly on cabin
TV 4	6104-8093-8136	59/0	3540	135	405	
TV 4B	6142-6157	54/0	3240	352	621	No lite in cabin, belt off
TV 4P	6280-2320	38/1	2440	403	753	
DE 8A	6150-7919-6048	60/20	5153	417	729	
GRB 22	6076-6098-6236-6083	100/0	13000	644	1010	
LH 14	5876	3/6	----	845(Jacks)	945(Lewis)	
AT 2	9023	2/0	160	824	945(Gray)	
CG 2	3180-6028-2335	A.M. 85/3	6160	902	1154	
Yard	9125	P.M. 20/3	----	1209(Hunt)	1232(Jacks)	
Work	8151	0/4	----	115	141Spruce)	
# 30	Amtrak 596-578	9	----	252	507	
RR 2	6192-6026	23/33	3038	200	538	
HE 2	6329	35/34	4091	200(Pete)	609	
TV 26	8089-2745-2875	44/0	3500	554	849	
AS 2	3222-6092-3174	50/35	5991	603	621(Gray)	
WPB 4	6206-6515-8083	69/15	5930	837	---	
TV 2	3132-3023-6507	67/0	4690	824	1207	
SW 6	8138-6514-6530	81/9	6540	849	---	
TV 20	6197-6186-7942-7911	68/0	4510	859	---	
XGP 6	8115-2259	0/115	3250	959	---	
CG 8	2263-2286-7716-6124	64/4	4420	1037	---	
CNY 4	7874-2524-2275	27/36	2855	1050	---	
TV 10-12	6270-3247-2446-8104	53/2	3780	1100	---	
OE 8	6013-6034	73/26	6060	1145	---	
AS 2	8101-2906	44/22	4877	1153	1226(Gray)	

Extraordinary or Unusual Occurrences

7:08am #40 589 hit pair of Dolly wheels at MP 148.5. #1 trk. Supvr notfd. Removed 735am, off trailer.
2:03pm Antis RR 2 6192 stopped east of Antis on #2. 8 deep PC 887762 ABCO. On move 222pm
10:50pm train wire noisy. Unable to use selector Also no tower east of Jacks. Wire chief notfd
11:50pm TV2 3132 just w of View #1 trk air in emergency. Kicker. Delay 10".
4:57pm track circuit east of View #2 trk out. C&S notfd. OK 535pm after #31
9:01pm TV20 6197 Stopped east of Antis to release brakes on 18th car TTX 254703, 23rd car TTX 473161 and 42nd car TTX 784048. Also closed door on 43rd car TTX 157289 N.S.
8:26pm TV2 3132 stopped east of Antis to release brakes & proceed. Will check at Gray. OK